PRAISE FOR MARK SINGER AND *THE SIX SECRETS TO A HAPPY RETIREME*

"A must-read for anyone going through reti
—*Ronnie Lott, N.*

"In a growing forest of retirement advice, *The Six Secrets to a Happy Retirement* offers practical short-cuts—financially, physically, and emotionally—for the journey. This slender book aims to help you travel light, with tips on avoiding unexpected taxes, knowing when to take your Social Security, getting fit, and de-cluttering your life of old furniture, real and emotional.

"For my money, the most critical secrets come condensed in a chapter by therapist/ coaches Dorian Mintzer and Roberta Taylor: how to have healthy talks, before any decisions are made, with your partner about your dreams and future needs for home, travel, money, sex, family or community. Read their good advice to get where you want to go with the one you love."

—*Bruce Frankel,*
author of What Should I Do With The Rest Of My Life? True Stories of
Finding Success, Passion and New Meaning in the Second Half of Life

"*The Six Secrets to a Happy Retirement*, edited by Mark Singer, is an invaluable resource for navigating the complicated life transitions of our Third Age. I particularly enjoyed and valued the chapters by Dorian Mintzer and Roberta Taylor on Retirement Conversations for Couples; Sallie Felton's chapter on How to be your Best from the Inside Out; and Kurt Czarnowski's chapter on Social Security and Retirement Planning. Add this book to your Third Age resource list!"

—*Olivia Mellan,*
money coach, psychotherapist and author of Money Harmony

"*The Six Secrets to a Happy Retirement* should be mandatory reading! The philosophy of addressing financial, emotional and physical issues before they become an issue is brilliant. The star-studded collection of authors share their expertise in a clear and concise way that makes it easy for the reader to follow along and therefore reap the rewards of learning the information."

—*Dr. Celina Spence*

"In this expert guide, Mark Singer explains the intricacies of retirement in clear, easy-to-understand language. The book is loaded with important, timely info that all of us can use starting now. And it goes well beyond just financial matters. It offers help in enjoying a 'happy retirement,' with the author addressing the emotional side of things that matter so much."

—Jordan Rich,
WBZ Radio Boston and CBS Radio

"Nobody can teach you how to retire. The journey is as varied as the human personality. But do read this book before you go. It's a clear, complete guide on what to pack and what to expect from an often-confusing terrain. Keep it handy in your travels, too, for it just might serve as a compass on a dark night."

—Susan Trausch,
author of Groping Toward Whatever or How I Learned to Retire, Sort Of

"For those approaching retirement or actually in retirement, this book is an excellent guide addressing all aspects of preparing for and living the good life in one's 'golden years.'

"As someone who teaches financial investing to this age group, I appreciate the value the book represents. The book is not only an easy read in terms of understanding but more important is a great guide on steps we can take to get the greatest joy out of this period of our lives."

—Larry Barrett

THE SIX SECRETS TO A HAPPY RETIREMENT

How to Master the Transition of a Lifetime

Mark Singer CFP®, editor

Contributors:
Erwin Allado
Kate Allado
Kurt Czarnowski
Sallie Felton
Peter Martone
Dorian Mintzer
Mark Singer
Roberta K. Taylor

ATA PRESS

Published by ATA Press
ISBN 978-0-9837620-6-5
Library of Congress Control Number 2013934323
First printing: March, 2013

All brand names and product names used in this book are trademarks, registered trademarks, or trade names of their respective holders. All statements contained herein
are the opinion of the author and should not be considered professional advice.

TABLE OF CONTENTS

TABLE OF FIGURES

INTRODUCTION

I have owned a retirement planning firm for 25 years, and many of my clients are now reaching retirement age. That's not surprising, but what I find interesting is how my conversations with them have changed. Instead of focusing on money, we now spend a lot more time talking about life itself.

During a recent conversation I was struck by just how important it really is, when one is considering the transition of retirement, to talk about much more than just the financial considerations. Let me share that conversation with you.

Joe had worked for a company for over 30 years. He was a guiding light for many of his peers, and was recognized as being someone who had helped shape the growth of the company. He had been looking forward to retirement for some time, and now that he had reached the age of 60 he was eligible to retire.

Joe and I had previously done a Retirement Roadmap, and it was clear that he could have a very enjoyable retirement. But when he came in with his wife to make the final decision, something interesting happened. Joe had been so focused on the numbers that he had yet to address the emotions that come with this transition. For the first time, he was faced with the reality of starting a new chapter in his life, and he was terrified.

Leaving a job is so much more than just leaving a paycheck. If you think about it, having a job means you have a reason to get up at a specified time in the morning, you have a certain routine that you have become accustomed to, and you have a workplace filled with people you spend as much time with as your own family members.

When you retire, you give up your routine, your place to "go to" and a place where you are a valuable contributor. In return, you receive respect and the knowledge that you are a part of a team. For some, it is like leaving home. It is so important to recognize this transition and to prepare yourself emotionally as well as financially. Take the time to prepare yourself and start early to visualize how you are going to move forward into the next chapter of your life.

It could be that you will spend more time with a particular passion. I have a friend who is retiring, and I was concerned about him because he really had no passions other than work. But he recently bought a '67 Corvette, and now that car is his baby. He is spending his retirement attending antique car shows regularly and hobnobbing with other Corvette owners, creating a new community of friends.

You may volunteer and end up contributing just as much as you were when you were working. Or you may decide to work part-time, creating a new reason to get up and be a constructive member of the community.

Most people spend more time researching an annual vacation than they do for their retirement. The biggest lesson I can possibly teach anyone is to approach retirement in much the same way you would approach planning a trip to Disney World.

When I went to Disney World with my daughter 17 years ago, I knew exactly which rides I would go on and when (yes, I bought the book that told me what to do), I knew how long I would stay, where I would stay, and how much the trip would cost.

For your retirement, do you know what your cash flow need is? Do you know how much risk to take with your money? Do you know how much you are going to spend traveling? Do you know how to minimize the taxes on the income you generate from your investments?

My objective for this book is to bring to you some of the experts in some of the areas that are so crucial to the success of this transition. My hope is that you come away understanding how to put yourself in the best possible position to truly enjoy your transition into retirement.

This book will address some of the financial, physical, and emotional issues many people face when they retire. To that end, I have assembled an all-star cast of contributors to share their insights with you.

Social Security is one of the major pieces of income we expect in retirement, and there certainly are many headlines indicating that the system has some serious issues. Kurt Czarnowski is a veteran of the Social Security Administration and recently retired himself, and he has written a chapter on not only how to maximize your benefits, but also knowing what some of the income options are for you and your spouse.

Communications are a key part to any relationship. And when one retires from working for 40 years, 50 hours a week, and suddenly that person is going to be home all day, the communications could become strained. Roberta Taylor and Dorian Mintzer have co-authored a nationally renowned book entitled *The Couples Retirement Puzzle*. They will be discussing some of the most important issues to talk about during this next phase of life.

And as we move on in life, we find that we have collected a lot of clutter along the way. Life coach, author, and international talk show host Sallie Felton helps us to deal with the emotional, mental, and physical clutter we have accumulated during our lifetime.

One chapter will talk about two of the most frequently asked questions I get as a Certified Financial Planner®. First, how do you know when you can retire? And second, once you have retired, how do you generate the income you'll need to lead your life? This chapter is an extension of the nationally acclaimed book I wrote last year, entitled *The Changing Landscape of Retirement — What You Don't Know Could Hurt You.*

Dr. Peter Martone has established himself as a pioneer in the world of fitness and nutrition. He founded a wellness center in the Boston metropolitan area, and he speaks nationally to other professionals of the wellness community, advising them how to bring the wellness conversation to their patients. He has a unique philosophy that I am sure will enlighten you as you endeavor to be the best you can be as a retiree.

One of the questions we get from our clients is about retirement living. Erwin and Kate Allado, owners of an Internet firm called SeniorCareHomes.com, have written a compelling chapter addressing two aspects of this critical subject: First, as you retire, you may want to find a new home for the next stage in your life. Second, as we retire, we may have to deal with parents who are aging. They write about some of the options for senior facilities for your folks.

I hope that when you finish the book you will understand, well beyond just the numbers, what it takes to establish the retirement of your dreams.

PART I

FINANCIAL
SECRETS

From a purely financial point of view, a successful retirement is driven by cash flow. The definition of a well-planned retirement is to do what you want to do when you want to do it, because you have enough cash flow to do it. However, too many people do not understand what they need to do to create the retirement of their dreams: Where will the money come from? How can I generate an income from my portfolio? What Social Security option is best for my family and me? They end up spending a lot of time worrying about spending the money "today" because they may not have enough money "tomorrow." The good news is that we are living longer; the bad news is that we may outlive our income stream in retirement. Instead of facing the issue head on and taking control, many people do no planning at all because they're afraid of what the answers may be.

In this section we'll answer some of the most important questions and reveal planning secrets that will help guide you toward your dream retirement.

CHAPTER 1:

ANSWERS TO THE TWO MOST IMPORTANT RETIREMENT QUESTIONS

Mark Singer CFP®

Question #1: Am I on track for a successful retirement, or will I run out of money?

One of the stories I tell my clients is the one about my daughter and her Great Train Adventure: When my daughter was 15, she went on her first train ride alone to a chorale rehearsal on the North Shore of Boston. Once the train pulled out of the station, the conductor came up and asked her for her ticket, which she gladly handed to him. Unfortunately for my daughter, the train she was on was going in the wrong direction. She was supposed to be on the northbound train, but she had boarded the southbound train! This was her first time on the train alone, so she was unaware of the fact that it was headed in the wrong direction. How was she to know? She had never done this before!

If you are thinking about transitioning into retirement, this is a first-time journey for you. And even though you may be headed towards "a destination," you may not know whether it is the "intended destination." Many of us just don't know what we don't know, and therein lies a huge problem. If you don't know what questions to ask, and most don't, then you may be on the southbound train when you are supposed to be headed north. It was easy for my daughter to get off the southbound train at the next stop and get onto the train headed in the right direction. Unfortunately, some of the mistakes that you may make when planning for your retirement will not be so easily reconcilable.

It is very important to recognize what you don't know because, without this information, you may make mistakes that will undermine your retirement.

One of the most important aspects of the transition into retirement is knowing when you can retire. One recent survey indicated that 24% of people have postponed their retirement date at least once in the past year. Another study by AARP revealed that 40% of Baby Boomers plan to "work until they drop." Why are we so fearful of retirement?

When our parents were retiring, they were relying on what we called the three-legged stool of retirement income.

The first leg was their pension. For many of our parents, they worked at one company, retired, and collected a well-deserved pension. This is no longer the norm. Not only are major companies changing the way their retirees are getting paid, but many are no longer offering pensions because of the cost of having to insure the future income needs of all of their employees.

The second leg was Social Security. When the Social Security system was implemented back in 1937, the landscape was very different. At that time there were many more people working and paying into the system than there were people retired and getting payments. Today, that equation has changed. 10,000 Baby Boomers a year are retiring, and the demand on the pool of money is much greater than it was previously.

We are also living longer now than we did 75 years ago. With more people retiring now, and drawing income for a much longer period of time, it is no wonder that we are reading about the financial crunch facing the Social Security system.

The third leg was our personal savings. The problem with this is that as we have gotten closer to retirement, the markets have not cooperated. We have been in a flat market (a secular bear market) for the past 12 years. And if history is our guide, this condition could last another three to five years.

Add to this the fact that as a general rule, our parents put their children (us) through college at a younger age than we did. Many of us had children later in life, and that meant that the expense of college came at a later age for us, meaning that we had more cash flow concerns, and debt, than our parents did when they were getting close to retirement.

So let's look at the difference between our parents' situation and ours. They could rely upon their pension and Social Security, get some help from their own savings, have little debt, and be all set for retirement. Their "retirement number" — the number they needed to have as their own savings — was typically much lower than ours is.

We, on the other hand, may have no pension, may have many concerns about the financial health of Social Security, may be experiencing a market that has not performed for an extended period of time, and may have significant debt if we educated our kids when we would normally have focused on planning for retirement.

It's little wonder that Baby Boomers are scared. Scared of running out of money.

Your Retirement Number

You've probably noticed the popular advertising campaign that introduces the concept of knowing what your "retirement number" is. The first iteration of images was of people who were carrying around seven-figure numbers under their arms, smiling along the way to their destination, and then putting their "retirement numbers" in nice safe places. With recent market volatility, these images have changed. Now you see someone walking in the street with the number under his or her arm, and the number gets hit by the bus and falls to the street. Or that same person is in a restaurant where the number is set on fire by the activities of the next table. Clearly the message has changed, indicating that there is now a rougher ride towards accomplishing your "retirement number."

The most recent image from this campaign is of an individual who is trimming the hedges, and above his head the words "gazillion bazillion" are in neon lights, symbolizing his "retirement number." When asked by his neighbor how he was going to accomplish his goal of achieving a gazillion bazillion dollars, the answer was that he was just going to continue to throw money as quickly as possible towards his retirement and see what happened.

This ad campaign has clearly captured what many people have felt at various times: a sense of hopelessness. One of the messages from the sponsor of this ad campaign is that you need to know what your number is and take the right steps to achieve it.

But from my perspective, as cute as these ads are, they do not address some of the very real problems and mistakes that people need to be aware of.

The first issue is that most of the people carrying numbers under their arms had numbers that were well into seven figures. The numbers that reflect their "retirement number" were upwards of $1.4 to $1.7 million. In my experience, when I tell somebody that they have to accumulate upwards of $1.7 million in order to have their correct "number," I usually get a "deer in the headlights" look as a response. Few people truly recognize how to save enough money, given all of the day-to-day issues we all face, towards a goal that may be many years away.

I would submit that the message should not have focused only on what your number is, but how to discipline yourself to put away that kind of money. It's important to know what "the number" is, but understanding what kind of risk we need to take and what time frame we have is equally important.

The second issue I have with this ad campaign is that it doesn't tell people what to do once they have accomplished their goals. One of the biggest mistakes I have found that most people make is that they continue to take more risk than is necessary with their investment portfolios, even after they have accomplished their "number." They often end up losing a significant portion of their retirement nest egg at just the wrong time.

Many years ago, I spoke with an individual who was six months away from retiring. He had enough saved in his retirement plan to create his desired retirement. That was the good news. The bad news was that his timing and planning could not have been worse. This was in the late 1980s, and he was working for a very successful organization called Wang. He thought that as a result of having invested 100% of his retirement savings in Wang stock, he was a financial genius.

If you're familiar with Wang, you know the rest of the story; two months before he was to retire, Wang stock dropped precipitously, devastating his retirement savings and rendering him unable to pursue the retirement he and his wife had dreamed of.

He is not alone. A couple of years ago I met a woman who was preparing for her retirement. She was in her early 60s and was planning to retire within the next two to three years. The good news was that she had accomplished her number — $1 million. The bad news was that neither she nor her broker knew what her number was. So what happened?

For all of her working life, she had been working with a series of brokers who had advised her to invest in such a way as to achieve as much growth as possible. While she was in her 30s and 40s, whether the market was going up or down was of little consequence because she had enough time to make up for a down market. Now, however, she was within a couple of years of retirement, and it was necessary for her to change the investment objectives.

But because neither she nor her broker understood that she had already accomplished her objectives, the portfolio remained with a growth orientation. In 2008, when the markets lost significant value, the $1 million portfolio dropped to $620,000, assuring that she could no longer retire as she had desired in two to three years.

Unfortunately, it was not until after the markets had dropped in 2008 that we had the opportunity to speak. And it was not until then that she understood the importance of having a Retirement Roadmap. If she had understood the concept of the Retirement Roadmap, she would have changed the objectives of her investment portfolio and geared it towards preservation rather than growth, potentially saving her portfolio tens of thousands of dollars in lost value. With a Retirement Roadmap, it would have been possible to retire according to her original plan. Without the Retirement Roadmap, neither she nor her broker understood that she was headed in the wrong direction.

Developing Your Retirement Roadmap

We often make decisions based on our emotions and how we "feel" about something. That's obvious in politics, sports, and our relationships, but it's also true when we talk about finances and retirement. I find that the people I talk to have often created visions of their retirement based more on their emotions (and often times that emotion is fear) than on the facts.

So let's understand some of the most important components of your Retirement Roadmap and why it is necessary to develop one so that you can pursue a successful retirement.

Just like planning your trip to Disney World, you need to think through some basic steps.

The most important step is understanding your cash flow needs. Cash flow is the number one driver of a successful retirement. You could be worth millions of dollars, but if you are not able to generate the income needed to live the lifestyle you desire, then you will not have a successful retirement.

Understand your monthly/annual cash flow needs. This is where all good retirement planning starts. Why? Because until you know your cash flow needs, you'll never know if you are taking on the correct amount of risk with the management of your money.

Here is an example for you: John and Lisa are about to retire, and have determined that they need a monthly income, net after taxes (very important to take taxes into consideration; many people forget this line item) of $6,000. They are going to receive $3,000 in Social Security and $2,000 in pensions. Therefore, they need to generate $1,000 per month from other sources. They could choose to pick up part-time jobs, but instead they have decided they do not want to work. Their portfolio, a $600,000 rollover IRA from John's 401(k), will have to generate the needed income.

Now that we know what income they need, we can model an appropriate portfolio construction. John and Lisa will have to generate a gross distribution of $14,000 annually in order to generate the net after-tax number of $12,000. This represents a 2.4% annual distribution. Assuming they want to keep up with inflation as the years go on, and if we assume that inflation will be 4%, they need a portfolio that will earn at least 6.4% annually. This will provide them with the right inflation-adjusted income for their retirement.

Instead of looking at the portfolio and guessing what investments are needed and not understanding the level of risk necessary, we can take on the appropriate allocation for the portfolio by starting from the cash flow analysis.

Too many people lost too much money by taking on more risk than they had to. Conversely, if you are so scared that you put all of your money in the bank, you will be taking on less risk than necessary and will more than likely run out of money.

With the use of the Retirement Roadmap, you'll learn when you can retire and how much risk you need to take with the portfolio in order to enjoy the rest of the journey.

Question #2: Now that I have accumulated enough assets to retire, how do I generate the income I need?

The world of financial planning is divided into two distinctive phases. The first phase is accumulation—while you are working. The goal is to put away as much money as possible and get the highest market returns so that you can accomplish your Retirement Number (see the previous section). This is the phase that we go through when we are working and have retirement as a distant goal, many years away.

The second is the distribution phase—while you are retired. The goal here is to generate the income needed to accomplish your desired lifestyle. And now that you are no longer working, and more than likely not contributing any more to your retirement accounts, preservation of your principal may be more important than growth.

The planning you need to do in each phase is very different. The accumulation phase focuses almost exclusively on growing money. Planning for the distribution phase encompasses cash flow, tax efficiencies, estate planning, and money management.

When you leave the workplace, you leave behind your paycheck. So the question becomes how to plan properly so that you can get the income you need, inflation adjusted, for the rest of your retirement? And even though the answer may be different for everyone, there is a four-step process that works the same for everyone.

1. Identify Your Ongoing Needs

In the last section we discussed the importance of cash flow analysis. The first step is to identify your ongoing expenses.

There are two general categories of expenses, fixed and discretionary. Fixed expenses include such things as the mortgage payment, car payments, utilities, groceries, insurance payments, and tax bills. Discretionary expenses include things like clothing, maintenance on the house or car, dining out, charitable giving, travel, and gifts. Of course, there may be other items depending on how you live your life.

One important rule of thumb is to add another 15% to the number you come up with. Most people are NOT able to capture ALL expenses, so it's important to build in a margin of error in the planning. You can annually check the expenses and make adjustments to the plan if necessary.

One line item I find many forget is taxes. If you need $100,000 per year spendable money, then you need to adjust your distributions to accommodate taxes. If you are taking income out of retirement accounts (IRAs, 401(k)s, annuities, 403(b)s) then you will have to withhold the correct amount of taxes.

There are many worksheets out there for you to use, so I'm not going to burden you with another here.

2. Identify Your Bucket List

In addition to the ongoing expenses mentioned above, there is your Bucket List. Those big-picture items are things you want to accomplish. They may include a new car, travel, painting the house, buying a second home, and much more.

The key to a successful Bucket List, particularly when it comes to the process of planning for retirement, is to be as specific as possible. For instance, "I want to travel" is different than "I want to travel to Italy in two years, for two weeks at a cost of $12,000." Why?

One of the important issues for those who are retired is, "If I spend the money today, will I have it tomorrow?" Well, when you quantify the Bucket List you actually take the mystery out. Let's look at an example in a bit more detail as it relates to the planning process.

You can put exact numbers into your plan and know one way or the other whether spending that money will have an impact on future cash flow issues. Your plan may indicate that you are all set, or it may suggest that you only need to spend $10,000, or that spending $12,000 may be an issue. Either way, you will know whether you are on the right track to accomplish your goal.

If you don't put in a specific number, there will always be a question as to whether or not it is okay to spend the money. Without a plan, without specifics, there will never be true clarity.

3. Set Up Emergency Reserves

It's important to have liquid money available in the event things happen beyond the norm, and they always seem to happen. So when it comes to proper planning, the first thing you want to establish is an emergency reserve. This is the "sleep at night" money. You want to feel comfortable that you can get your hands on money quickly, and not have to liquidate something within your investment portfolio in the event of an emergency.

For many of my clients, that number is typically somewhere between $30,000 and $60,000. For some it's lower, and for a handful it can be as high as $100,000. You don't want to sell something at just the wrong time within your portfolio if something out of the ordinary happens and you need the money. So the more the emergency reserves, the less will be "working" in the portfolio. Finding the right balance for you may take some time as you go through the transition into retirement.

Once you have established your emergency reserve, the rest of the money should be working within your overall investment strategy. There is always going to be a tradeoff, and you must understand this—the money earmarked for the emergency reserves will not be earning money. Its only goal is to be available immediately, if needed.

4. Generating the Income Tax-Efficiently

The real trick to generating the income you need is to identify which accounts will generate how much income and when. To do this properly, and to generate the most tax-efficient income, you must integrate different aspects of the planning process. Your plan should incorporate things like asset allocation, cash flow analysis, taxes, and retirement distribution rules.

Let's set up a case study to understand exactly how this works. George and Karen have $900,000 in their investment portfolio. $300,000 is in an IRA rollover and $600,000 is in a personal, taxable account. George is 66 and retiring at the end of the year; Karen is retired already.

They have determined that they need $8,000 per month, net after taxes. They are collecting $3,200 net from Social Security and another $3,000, net after taxes, in a monthly pension from Karen's previous employer. This means that the portfolio will have to generate $1,800 net. Additionally, they have set aside $40,000 for their emergency reserve.

The question they face is which account should they generate the needed income from, now and in the future? For now, the answer is from their personal portfolio. George is not yet 70½, the age he must start to take Required Minimum Distributions (RMD), therefore he does not need to take money out of his IRA. This is important from a tax perspective, because any distributions from the IRA will be taxed at their ordinary income rate. If George and Karen make the proper investment allocation decisions, this rate will be higher than taking income from the personal account.

So for the first four years of George's retirement, they should plan to take the necessary $1,800 from his personal account. Then when he reaches 70½, he will be forced to take out approximately 3.6% of the value of the IRA at that time.

We know that George needs $1,800 monthly, which represents 3.6% of the total of his personal portfolio. In the traditional method of income production, George could allocate attractive income-producing investments that would generate the income needed. He could be conservative with the personal portfolio, and use more growth-oriented investments within the IRA.

In so doing, George would have a well-balanced portfolio. The more conservative portfolio in the personal account would be earmarked to provide income, while the IRA would be earmarked for growth.

Then when George reaches 70½ and has to make the RMD, he can reduce the income generated from the personal portfolio. And now that the personal portfolio has to generate less income (because the IRA is getting him income from the RMD), he can reduce his tax exposure by moving some of the income-oriented investments to more growth-oriented investments, or look at alternatives that could defer the income for him.

The important take-away here is to understand that you need to coordinate various aspects of the planning process in order to get the most tax-efficient income possible in retirement.

Three Methods of Income Distribution

There are various methods of setting up your portfolio to generate the income you need. By now you understand that without going through the proper planning steps, you may not know exactly what income to draw from where.

Unlike many of my financial planning peers, I think that setting up your portfolio is one of the last items to address. Until you know what your cash flow need is and what your Bucket List items are, you can't possibly know how much risk to take with your portfolio. And, as seen in the case study, you can actually reduce your tax burden by coordinating what investments are owned in which accounts. That of course will depend on how many accounts you have (retirement versus personal) and how old you are. By developing your own personalized Retirement Roadmap, you can truly take the mystery out of many of the decisions you will need to make during the transition into retirement.

So let's take a look at some of the mechanics of setting up your portfolio to get the income you need.

The first method is the traditional one detailed in the case study above: Identify the accounts you need to draw your income from, and then distribute the income/dividends to cover your income needs. There are a number of investments, both on the equity and fixed income side, so a comprehensive knowledge of these investments is vital.

Be wary of going after unusually high yields. If it walks like a duck and talks like a duck...well, you know the rest. If you see that most bonds are paying 3%, and one is paying 6%, you need to do some research before you buy it to understand what the tradeoffs are. Is it higher risk? Is there a longer duration? Is there some limited liquidity? There is going to be something that differentiates it from its peers. Understand these things before going in.

The second method is one I use with many of my clients. Once you understand how much your portfolio must generate — say for a random example $22,000 per year — then you can set aside one to two years' income in a cash account and draw that down on a monthly basis. For two years, you would move $44,000 into the cash account. At the end of the one or two years, you evaluate the line items in the portfolio, sell enough to replenish the cash for another one- or two-year period, and start again.

By setting aside the correct amount in the cash account, you don't have to worry about whether the markets are up or down. In volatile times, it may be detrimental to sell during a down time to generate your income needs, so doing it this way you don't have to sell any of your investments or use the dividends. You'll have more time for the investments to perform as they should.

The third method has become more popular of late, particularly if you are planning for income later. This method is not for everyone; however, in the right situation, it can add a lot of value to the income planning process.

If you have enough income for now but are concerned about income in the future, you may want to find out about some of the living benefits within some of the annuity companies.

Annuities have been a popular retirement product for years, but I have not used them very much in my practice. I believe many are too expensive and have limited investment features. However, some of the annuities are now offering some very attractive living benefits.

By allocating a portion of your portfolio (no more than 15%-20%) to an annuity that offers a future income rider, you may be better off down the road.

For example, let's say you want to add income in 10 years. You select a living benefit that would pay you a guaranteed income starting in 10 years for the rest of your life. During these first 10 years, while you don't need to draw income, you can take on more risk with the portfolio than you would if you didn't have future guarantees. With an annuity, you are guaranteed a certain income for life based on the amount you originally invest.

The beauty of this is that if the portfolio does not perform well, you are still guaranteed the income based on the amount you originally put in, but if the value of your portfolio is higher in 10 years, then you could actually receive more income. Again, I do not recommend this for everyone; however, in the right circumstances, it could be a good value-add for your portfolio.

Conclusion

The key to understanding how to generate the income you need for retirement lies in planning. If you really wish to put yourself in the best position to pursue a successful retirement, approach this like you would your trip to Disney World.

Step back, set your goals, put together your personalized Retirement Roadmap, and align your portfolio with your income needs. In this way, you will know whether or not you are on the right track to enjoy the rest of your life.

Questions to Consider

Do you know when you can retire? Have you developed the Retirement Roadmap that will help you determine the optimum date?

Are you taking on the correct amount of risk with your investments in order to generate the cash you need for your retirement journey?

Have you set up the proper income flow from your portfolio so that you can minimize your tax exposure?

Are you utilizing the four-step process to establish the financial peace of mind needed for your retirement cash flow?

Have you coordinated your retirement goals with your investment objectives so that you don't lose more money than you should?

Have you spent more time planning your vacation to Disney World than you do for your retirement?

Have you updated your portfolio to reflect what is happening in today's uncertain markets?

Are you aware of some of the little-known investments that were previously available only to the super-wealthy?

About the Author

Mark Singer has created the "Retirement Roadmap" and the "Financial Organizer System," both of which have helped thousands of investors successfully coordinate their financial affairs.

Mark is the author of the nationally acclaimed book *The Changing Landscape of Retirement – What You Don't Know Could Hurt You*, and is a frequent speaker and founder of the Greater Boston Corporate Wellness Forum. Over the past 25 years, he has produced several radio and television shows that have focused on providing solutions to retirees.

He is recognized nationally by numerous media outlets as a retirement planning expert, and has appeared in *The Wall Street Journal*, and on ABCNews.com, FoxNews.com, and Bloomberg Radio, as well as locally (Boston) on NECN and WRKO, among others.

The success of Mark's retirement planning firm can be attributed to its core mission of addressing his clients' total needs. These conversations are much more than the traditional stocks-and-bonds approach of many of his peers. As a result, he is recognized in Boston as one of the leading retirement planners in the region.

To learn more about Mark and his books, and to download free retirement worksheets, visit www.yourretirementjourney.com.

CASH FLOW WORKSHEET

Income	Monthly	Annual
Salary		
Average Commission		
Bonus		
Part-Time Work		
Self-Employment Income		
Interest/Dividends		
Alimony		
Pension		
Social Security		
Other		
GROSS INCOME		

Deductions/Fixed Expenses	Monthly	Annual
Federal Taxes		
State Taxes		
Real Estate Taxes		
Social Security Taxes		
Group Benefits		
Mortgage/Rent		
Life Insurance		
Health Insurance		
Auto/Home Insurance		
Disability/Long-Term Care Insurance		

Deductions/Fixed Expenses	Monthly	Annual
Alimony/Child Support		
Tuition/Education		
Groceries/Personal Care		
Gas/Electric/Water		
Telephone/Cable/Internet		
Car Payments		
Savings/Investments		
Retirement Contributions		
Other		
TOTAL FIXED EXPENSES		

Variable Expenses	Monthly	Annual
Clothing		
Medical/Drugs/Dental		
Auto Repair/Maintenance		
Home Repair/Maintenance		
Dining Out/Entertainment		
Gas/Public Transportation		
Gifts		
Vacation/Travel		
Donations/Charitable Giving		
Other		
TOTAL VARIABLE EXPENSES		

TOTAL EXPENSES
(fixed + variable)

Total Net Cash Flow	Monthly	Annual
Total Gross Income (from above)		
Total Fixed Expenses (enter as negative)		
Total Variable Expenses (enter as negative)		
TOTAL NET INCOME (discretionary)		

YOUR BUCKET LIST

With your retirement years just around the corner, doesn't it make sense to get some of your secret thoughts down on paper to make them real?

People always say, "Of course I want to _____, but I just can't afford to do it." Maybe you're right, maybe you just don't have the money, but do you know that for sure? Have you ever sat down and truly crunched the numbers?

For now, let's keep it simple. Print out this page and start to think about your dream activities. Jot them down in the space provided, and then take a step back to examine the list. You may be surprised at what you see... and the truth is, you may also be able to accomplish these goals with the money you've saved — you just don't know it yet!

Remember to be as specific as you can. A trip to Italy is a good item on the Bucket List; however, a trip in two years that will last two weeks and cost about $12,000 is much more specific. This will not only help you to visualize it better, but also to put it into your Retirement Roadmap. By putting it in the Roadmap, it will take the mystery out of the question as to whether or not by spending money on this trip it will impact your other retirement goals. Good luck!

CHAPTER 2

SOCIAL SECURITY AND RETIREMENT PLANNING

Kurt Czarnowski

Introduction

Social Security has been a basic part of American life for more than 76 years now, and each month more than 55 million people receive over $62B in benefit payments from it. And yet, despite the age, the size, and the economic impact of the Social Security system, the myths and misunderstandings about what the program is—and what it isn't—are legion.

It is particularly important that these myths and misunderstanding be addressed today, because nearly 75 million Baby Boomers will be reaching retirement age in the next 20 or so years. And these Boomers are approaching a retirement world far different from the one their parents and grandparents knew. If Boomers retire with any type of pension at all, it is more likely to be the defined contribution type (401(k), 403(b), and 457) than the traditional defined benefit type. Instead of being able to count on a guaranteed stream of income for life, Boomers are more likely to be retiring with a pile of money, and the onus is on them to make it last through their retirement. Compounding this problem is the fact that the economic downturn of the past few years has meant that these piles of money are probably not as large as they once were.

With this shift taking place in the retirement world, it is no surprise that a 2011 survey done by the Associated Press and LifeGoesStrong.com found that 65% of Boomers surveyed now say that they will be counting on Social Security as the cornerstone of their retirement income. However, many of them are now also waking up to the fact that they don't know as much about the system as they should.

What do Boomers need to know? First and foremost, they need to understand that Social Security was never intended to be a sole source of income in retirement. Instead, it is meant to be the foundation upon which to build a secure retirement. Social Security represents a base of income protection that people can count on, but it is a base which must be supplemented if people are going to achieve the type of retirement they desire. Unfortunately, Social Security represents almost the only source of income 24% of retirees receive on a monthly basis.

It doesn't matter how you supplement your Social Security benefits. You may have a traditional defined pension, a defined contribution plan, or other types of savings and investments, or even part-time work in retirement—all of these represent important ways to supplement your Social Security benefits.

The key to your retirement is understanding what Social Security provides, as well as what it doesn't provide. And one of the best ways to understand what the program will provide is by using the Social Security Administration's online Retirement Estimator: www.SocialSecurity.gov/estimator. The online estimator is an easy-to-use financial planning tool that allows you to get immediate and personalized retirement benefit estimates. Unlike other calculators, the online Retirement Estimator eliminates the need for you to manually key in years of earnings information. By changing your "stop work" dates or expected future earnings, you can create numerous "what if" scenarios to help you compare different retirement options and plan for your retirement.

How You Become Eligible for Retirement Benefits

You are eligible for Social Security benefits if you have worked in a job where Federal Insurance Contributions Act (FICA) tax has been deducted from your pay. These days, about 95% of the jobs in the country fall under the Social Security umbrella, with the largest group of non-covered workers being public employees in a number of jurisdictions, including the Commonwealth of Massachusetts. You also qualify if you are self-employed and have paid FICA tax on the net profit from your business.

However, in order to qualify for a Social Security retirement benefit, you need to have earned 40 Social Security "credits" throughout your working life. Each year, Social Security credits are earned based on a specific amount of earnings subject to Social Security tax. The amount required for a credit changes from year to year. In 2013, for example, you earn one credit for each $1,160 you make. You can earn a maximum of four credits in a year, so with earnings or a net profit of $4,640 or more in 2013, you garner four credits, regardless of when the money was earned.

The bottom line is that once you have accumulated 40 credits, you will definitely qualify for something when the time comes. Without 40 credits, however, you cannot receive anything based on your own work record, although you may be eligible for something based on the work and earnings of a spouse. This aspect of the program will be covered a bit later.

When to Start Receiving Retirement Benefits

These days, the most frequently asked question about Social

Security is "When should I start to collect my benefits?" Under the program, you have many options, but it is really up to you to decide which one makes the most sense. However, before deciding what you should do, you need to fully understand what you *can* do, and to begin that process you have to know what is considered your Full Retirement Age (FRA) for Social Security benefit purposes. (Your FRA is the earliest age at which an unreduced retirement benefit can be paid to you.) Incidentally, you may hear the term Normal Retirement Age used in this context, but I prefer the term Full Retirement Age. These days, there really is no normal retirement age, if there ever was one, because everyone's situation is different.

When Social Security started back in 1935, FRA was 65 for everyone, but in 1983 the law changed. That has meant an increase in FRA for anyone born in 1938 or later. For a large number of Baby Boomers, those born between 1943 and 1954, FRA is age 66. But it continues to increase for people born after 1954 and, under current law, for anyone born in 1960 or later, full retirement benefits are payable at age 67. The chart below lists the full retirement age by year of birth.

But starting to collect at FRA is not the only option you have, because you can begin to collect as early as age 62 if you choose to.

Figure 1:
Age to Receive
Full Social
Security
Benefits

Note: People who were born on January 1 of any year should refer to the previous year.

Year of Birth	Full Retirement Age
1943-1954	66
1955	66 and 2 months
1956	66 and 4 months
1957	66 and 6 months
1958	66 and 8 months
1959	66 and 10 months
1960 and later	67

However, Congress has built certain social goals into the program. One of these is a hope that you will collect roughly the same total amount of lifetime benefits, regardless of when you start to receive them. Therefore, if you begin to collect prior to the attainment of your FRA, your monthly payment will be reduced by roughly half a percentage point for each month that you collect a payment early. The rationale for this actuarial reduction is that if you start to collect prior to FRA, you will be collecting for a longer period of time, and so the amount you get each month is reduced. Incidentally, this is also a permanent reduction. Many people understand that if they start to collect early, they will receive a lower monthly amount. However, many of them also mistakenly believe that their payment will be automatically increased when they reach FRA. This is incorrect.

If you wait until your FRA to begin collecting, you will receive 100% of the amount your work and earnings have entitled you to receive. And, with the Social Insurance idea still in effect, if you choose to defer collecting past your FRA, your monthly benefit is increased in recognition of that. These increases are referred to as Delayed Retirement Credits (DRCs), and these days, your benefit amount is increased by two-thirds of a percent per month for each month past your FRA that you don't draw a payment. This means that your benefit will increase by 8% for each year that you don't collect, although it is important to note that DRCs stop accruing at age 70.

Incidentally, you never *have* to collect your Social Security benefits. There is no equivalent to the Minimum Required Distribution, but you gain no additional increase by waiting past age 70. Benefit amounts can, however, increase past age 70 because of additional work, or due to a Cost of Living Adjustment (COLA), and we will touch on this later.

The following chart provides an example of how your monthly

benefit amount can differ based on the age at which you decide to start receiving benefits:

Let's say your full retirement age is 66 and your monthly benefit starting at that age is $1,000. If you choose to start getting benefits at age 62, your monthly benefit will be reduced by 25% to $750 to account for the longer period of time you will receive benefits. This is generally a permanent reduction in your monthly benefit.

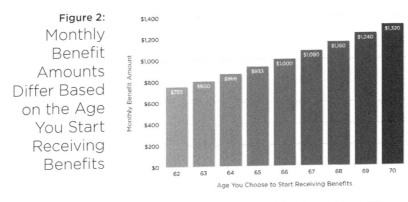

Figure 2:

Monthly Benefit Amounts Differ Based on the Age You Start Receiving Benefits

Note: This example assumes a benefit of $1,000 at a full retirement age of 66.

If you choose not to receive benefits until age 70, you will increase your monthly benefit amount to $1,320. This increase is from delayed retirement credits that you'll get for your decision to postpone receiving benefits past your full retirement age. The benefit amount at age 70 in this example is 32% more than you would receive per month if you chose to start getting benefits at full retirement age.

Today, more and more people are recognizing that this deferral strategy is one way to maximize their Social Security benefits. If you begin collecting benefits at 62, when you first become eligible, you'll get only 75% of what you would receive at Full Retirement Age, but if you wait until age 70, you'll get 132% of this same amount. From 75% at age 62 to 132% at 70 represents close to a doubling of the monthly retirement income that you will have for the rest of your life.

Obviously there are a number of factors you will need to consider in deciding when to start collecting your benefits. These will include things like your health, longevity, income taxes, and whether or not you need the money. In the end, though, it is up to you to decide what you should do.

Who lives to average life expectancy these days? As longevity increases, you may find yourself spending 20, 25, or perhaps even 30 years in retirement. In fact, a recent Social Security Administration study found that of today's 65-year-olds, one in four will live to age 90, and one in ten will live to age 95. In deciding when to start collecting, perhaps the better question to ask yourself is not "How do I get the most money today?" but "How do I ensure that I have enough money to last throughout my entire retirement?" And, for many people, the need for money may be more acute later in retirement, as health care costs will likely be higher and assets are more likely to have been depleted. Armed with this information, it may make more sense to defer, if you can. But again, it is your decision to make.

How Social Security Calculates a Benefit Amount

If "When should I start?" is the most frequently asked question, then "How is my benefit figured?" is probably the second most often asked. The Social Security Administration (SSA) calculates your monthly benefit amount using a formula that Congress has included in the Social Security Act. The amount you ultimately receive under the formula is tied to your work and earnings, and the higher your earnings have been, the more you receive on a monthly basis. Therefore, if there were some years when you did not work, or if you had low earnings, then your benefit amount may be lower than if you had worked steadily. In addition, only the earnings that were subject to Social Security tax are used in calculating your benefit. In other words, you only get credit for earnings up to the taxable maximum amount for each year. In 2013, if you had earnings (or Net Income from Self-Employment) of $500,000, you would only pay Social Security tax on $113,700, and this amount would ultimately be used in figuring your payment.

In calculating your benefit Social Security will first adjust, or index, your prior earnings for inflation. Social Security brings them up to what they are in today's dollars in order to account for changes in average wages since they were received. Because Congress has decided that benefits should be based on your lifetime earnings, Social Security then averages them over your highest 35 years of work, not just your "High 3" or "Last 5," like some other pension systems. A formula is then applied to these earnings to determine the basic benefit, or "primary insurance amount" (PIA), which is the amount you will receive at your full retirement age.

Another example of the Social Insurance aspect of the program is the fact that the benefit computation formula is designed to be a progressive, or weighted one. While there is a relationship between taxes paid and the monthly benefit received, Congress has recognized that people in lower-paying jobs are less likely to have a private pension to supplement their Social Security benefit. They are also less likely to be able to save, because they need their money for food clothing and shelter. Therefore, the system is set up to help people in lower-paying jobs by providing them with a monthly benefit intended to replace about 56% of their pre-retirement income. Higher wage earners receive more on a monthly basis, but their payments actually replace a lower percentage of their pre-retirement income, somewhere in the neighborhood of 34%.

Social Security payments are only intended to replace about 40% of pre-retirement income, and many financial experts say you will need 70-80% of your pre-retirement income to have a comfortable retirement. Again, Social Security was never intended to be someone's sole source of income in retirement. It has always been intended to provide a solid base of income protection, but it is a base that must be supplemented.

Spousal, Divorced Spousal, and Survivor's Benefits

As mentioned before, if you haven't earned 40 Social Security credits, you cannot collect a retirement benefit based on your own work record. However, it is possible to collect a payment based on the work and earnings of your spouse.

At your Full Retirement Age, you will be eligible to collect a benefit equal to 50% of your spousal Full Retirement Age amount, regardless of the amount he or she may actually be collecting. The earliest age that you can collect benefits as a spouse is age 62, but if you begin collecting before you have reached your Full Retirement Age, the amount of the benefit is reduced. For example, if your Full Retirement Age is 66, and you begin to collect spousal benefits at age 62, you will get 35 percent of the worker's unreduced benefit amount. It is important to note that if you are still married, you cannot receive spousal benefits until the higher earner has actually filed for retirement benefits.

If you have earned 40 credits but have had low earnings throughout your working life, it may be possible to collect a spousal benefit in addition to your own. If you are eligible for both your own retirement benefits and spousal benefits, you will generally receive your own benefits first. (See the following section on "Strategies for Maximizing Your Benefits" for an exception to this rule.) If your own benefit is higher than half of your spousal, then that's all you will receive. However, if your benefits as a spouse—i.e. one-half of the retired worker's full benefit amount—are higher than your own retirement benefits, you will get a combination of benefits equaling the higher spouse benefit.

Two last points about spousal benefits: First, the program is completely gender-neutral, and works the same way whether the higher earner is the husband or wife. Second, because of the federal Defense of Marriage Act, or DOMA, the Social Security Administration does not currently recognize same-sex marriages for benefit payment purposes.

If you are a divorced spouse, you can collect on your ex-spousal record if the marriage lasted at least 10 years and if you are at least age 62 and currently unmarried. If you have been divorced for at least two years, you can get benefits even if your ex-spouse is not yet entitled to benefits. However, he or she must be at least age 62, as well.

As a divorced spouse, you will be eligible to collect the higher of up to 50% of your ex's full benefit amount, or your own amount. The amount that you receive will have no effect on the amount of benefits that anyone else might be eligible to receive on your ex-spouse's work record.

While spouses can collect up to 50% of the full benefit amount, at FRA a widow or widower can collect up to 100% of what the deceased had been collecting. Widows and widowers can begin collecting a survivor's benefit as early as age 60, but once again collecting prior to FRA means the monthly benefit will be reduced. For example, a widow or widower who begins collecting at age 60 receives 71.5% of what he or she would have received by waiting until FRA.

As mentioned before, spousal benefits are a percentage of what the worker would have received at FRA rather than the amount he or she may actually be receiving. However, survivor's benefits are increased if the deceased worker had waited beyond FRA to begin collecting, and they do incorporate any Delayed Retirement Credits earned.

This leads to an important point to keep in mind when deciding when to start receiving retirement benefits: By collecting prior to FRA, not only is your own benefit reduced, but any survivor benefits that might eventually be paid are reduced as well. And by deferring past your FRA, both your own benefit amount and any survivor benefit is higher.

Strategies for Maximizing Social Security Benefits

There are three strategies couples can employ as a way to maximize the Social Security benefits they receive: "File and Suspend," "Claim Some Now—Claim More Later," and "The Combined Strategy."

In the **"File and Suspend"** strategy, the Primary Worker must be at or over Full Retirement Age. He or she applies for retirement benefits and then immediately requests that the benefit payments be suspended. This means that he or she will receive no benefit payments, but will begin to earn Delayed Retirement Credits. Now, because he or she has applied for benefits, the other member of the couple can apply for spousal benefits and begin to receive up to 50% of the FRA amount. The spouse must be at least age 62 to take advantage of this strategy, which became possible following the passage of the Senior Citizen's Freedom to Work Act back in the year 2000.

EXAMPLE: *Ward is at his FRA of 66, and at this point is eligible for $1,000 per month. His spouse, June, is 62 and has never worked outside the home. Because he is at his FRA, Ward can file an application for retirement benefits and then request that his payments be "suspended." Since June is age 62, and Ward has now applied, she can now collect spousal benefits. Because she is under her FRA, her benefit will be reduced and she will receive $350 per month, not the full 50% of Ward's amount. Ward will receive nothing at present, but he will earn*

Delayed Retirement Credits of 8% per year going forward. If he waits until age 70 to collect, his payment at that point will be $1,320 per month. Since June's spousal benefit is based on Ward's FRA amount, she will still receive only $350 per month when he begins to collect. But if Ward passes away, she will begin to receive $1,320 per month, because her widow's payment is based on what Ward has actually been collecting.

The **"Claim Some Now — Claim More Later"** strategy applies when your spouse is at least age 62 and has already applied for retirement benefits. If you have reached your full retirement age and are eligible for a spousal or ex-spousal benefit and your own retirement benefit, you may choose to receive only spousal benefits and earn Delayed Retirement Credits on your own Social Security record. You can then file for your own retirement benefits at a later date and receive a higher monthly payment based on the effect of the DRCs. You must be at or over your Full Retirement Age to employ this strategy, because prior to FRA, you cannot restrict the scope of your application and are "deemed" to file for your own benefit first.

EXAMPLE: *Ward and June have both worked under Social Security and each one would be eligible for $1,000 per month at FRA. Both reach FRA of 66 in the same month, and Ward decides to collect on his own, while June decides to wait. Ward will collect his $1,000, but because she is at her FRA, June can apply for only a spousal benefit and begin to receive $500 per month. Because she has not applied for her own retirement benefit, she will earn DRCs of 8% per year going forward. Later, at age 70, June can apply for her own benefit and begin to receive $1,320 per month. Incidentally, she doesn't have to wait* *until age 70 to apply on her own; she can begin to collect at whatever point makes the most sense to her, but there are no additional DRCs past age 70.*

As the name implies, the **"Combined Strategy"** utilizes features of the previous two. Here, both spouses must be at or over FRA, and one of them "files and suspends" while the other one applies for spousal benefits only. This allows some benefits to be paid while both members of the couple earn DRCs going forward. If the couple is still married, both members CANNOT receive only spousal benefits at the same time. However, divorced couples can, as long as the divorce was finalized at least two years previously.

EXAMPLE: *Ward and June have both worked, both are at their FRA of 66, and each one is entitled to collect $1,000 per month. Ward files for retirement benefits, and then requests that his payments be suspended. At the same time, June applies for "spousal benefits only." Because Ward has requested that his payments be suspended, he receives no monthly benefit. However, June immediately begins to collect $500 per month as a spouse. In addition, both of them earn DRCs of 8% per year, so their benefit amounts at age 70 will be $1,320 per month. Again, both of them cannot both "file and suspend" and collect a "spousal benefit only" at the same time.*

Work in Retirement

As Baby Boomers reach retirement age, many of them want to remain connected to the workforce in some fashion, so it is important to understand how work activity impacts your ability to collect Social Security benefits.

The good news is that once you have attained your FRA, there is no earnings limitation in place, and you can earn as much as you like and still collect a full Social Security benefit each month. However, if you collect benefits prior to your FRA, you can only make up to a certain amount each year before SSA begins to reduce your monthly benefit by $1 for each $2 you earn over the threshold. Note that only earned income (i.e. wages and/or net income from self-employment) counts towards the threshold. The receipt of unearned income, like a private pension, 401(k) distributions, bank interest, or dividends, does not impact your ability to collect a Social Security benefit each month. This earnings threshold generally increases every year, and in 2013, you are allowed to make up to $15,120 without any loss in benefits.

Whenever you work in a job covered by Social Security, your employer must deduct your Social Security and Medicare taxes from your salary and pay the equal employer's share of the taxes. This is true regardless of your age or retirement status. If you are self-employed while collecting benefits and the annual net profit from your business is more than $400, then that, too, is covered by Social Security and Medicare taxes. You must report those earnings and pay the Social Security and Medicare taxes when you file your personal income tax return.

The good news is that if you continue to work in retirement, SSA will automatically recompute your benefit amount each year, and your monthly payment will be increased if the prior year's earnings are now one of your highest 35 years. Any increase will be made retroactive to January of the year following the year you had the earnings. It is important to note that additional work in retirement will never reduce your monthly benefit amount. If your earnings happen to be lower than any of the 35 years that have been used up until that point, your benefit simply stays the same.

Taxation of Benefits

Prior to 1983, Social Security benefits were completely tax free, but now up to 85% of the benefits which you receive may be subject to federal income tax. Today about one-third of the people who get Social Security have to pay income taxes on their benefits.

If you file a federal tax return as an "individual," and the sum of your adjusted gross income, plus nontaxable interest, plus one-half of your Social Security benefits is between $25,000 and $34,000, you may have to pay taxes on 50 percent of your Social Security benefits. If this figure is more than $34,000, then up to 85 percent of your Social Security benefits is subject to federal income tax.

For a couple filing a joint return, if the sum of your adjusted gross income, tax-free interest, and one-half of your Social Security benefits is between $32,000 and $44,000, then you may have to pay taxes on 50 percent of your benefits. If this total is more than $44,000, then up to 85 percent of your Social Security benefits will be subject to income tax. (If you are married and file a separate return, you will probably pay taxes on your benefits.)

At the end of each year, you will receive a Social Security Benefit Statement (Form SSA-1099) that will show you the amount of benefits you received. You can use this statement when you complete your federal income tax return to find out if you have to pay taxes on your benefits.

Although you are not required to have federal taxes withheld from your Social Security benefit, you can ask to have it done. In order to have federal taxes withheld, you will need to: 1) complete an IRS Form W-4V, 2) select the percentage (7, 10, 15, or 25 percent) of your monthly benefit amount you want withheld, and 3) sign and return the form to your local Social Security office. You may obtain IRS Form W-4V from the IRS Website or by calling the IRS toll-free number, 1-800-829-3676.

Cost of Living Adjustment (COLA)

A hallmark of the Social Security program is that it is one of the few remaining Defined Benefit pension systems in the country today. This means that it is impossible to outlive your Social Security benefits, and you will receive a monthly benefit from the time you become eligible until the month you pass away. In addition, Social Security also provides a measure of inflation protection, which is becoming increasingly important as people are living longer and longer in retirement.

Prior to 1975, Social Security beneficiaries would receive periodic increases in their benefit payments if the increases were voted in by Congress. However, since 1975 beneficiaries have been guaranteed an annual Cost of Living Adjustment (COLA) based on changes in the Consumer Price Index for Urban Wage Earners and Clerical Workers (CPI-W). This is a measure of inflation maintained by the Federal Bureau of Labor Statistics (BLS), and it tracks the change in prices for a basket of goods and services.

From 1975 until 1982, COLAs were effective with Social Security benefits payable for June in each of those years; thereafter COLAs have been effective with benefits payable for December. In determining the annual increase in benefits, Social Security compares the average CPI-W for the third quarter of one year (July–September) to that of the prior year. The Administration announces the annual COLA in mid-October of each year, and any corresponding increase shows up in the benefit payments the following January.

Some people have argued that the CPI-W does not track the right things or is simply not a correct measure to use in determining benefit increases for a program which assists a large number of elderly people. But until Congress changes the law, it will be the measure used to determine the annual COLA, and it continues to be a vitally important part of the Social Security program.

Filing for Benefits

When it comes time to apply for benefits, you have options. You can apply for retirement benefits online by visiting the Social Security Administration's website: www.SocialSecurity.gov. More and more people are choosing this option these days. Social Security's online retirement application can be completed in as little as 15 minutes, from the comfort of your home or office, at a time most convenient for you. In most cases, once your application has been submitted electronically, you are all done. There are no forms to sign and usually no documentation required.

Figure 3:
Social Security Cost of Living Adjustments

Year	COLA	Year	COLA	Year	COLA
1975	8.0	1988	4.0	2001	2.6
1976	6.4	1989	4.7	2002	1.4
1977	5.9	1990	5.4	2003	2.1
1978	6.5	1991	3.7	2004	2.7
1979	9.9	1992	3.0	2005	4.1
1980	14.3	1993	2.6	2006	3.3
1981	11.2	1994	2.8	2007	2.3
1982	7.4	1995	2.6	2008	5.8
1983	3.5	1996	2.9	2009	0.0
1984	3.5	1997	2.1	2010	0.0
1985	3.1	1998	1.3	2011	3.6
1986	1.3	1999	2.5	2012	1.7
1987	4.2	2000	3.5		

However, if you are not comfortable applying online, you can also apply by calling Social Security's toll-free number, 1-800-772-1213. You can also apply in person by visiting any local Social

Security office, but it is best to call ahead to make an appointment.

Collecting Payments

Prior to May 1997, all regular monthly Social Security payments were made on the third of the month (or on the first prior business day whenever the third was not a business day). Since that time, however, benefit payments have also been made on the second, third, and fourth Wednesdays, respectively, of each month, regardless of the date. Beneficiaries whose birthdays are on or before the 10th of the month receive their benefits on the second Wednesday, those born on the 11th through the 20th receive theirs on the third Wednesday, and the rest receive theirs on the fourth Wednesday.

Since May 2011, the Treasury Department has required all new retirees to receive their monthly payments electronically, either by direct deposit to a bank or credit union account or to a Direct Express® Debit MasterCard® card account. The Treasury is phasing out paper check payments and by March 1, 2013, all federal benefit recipients will have to receive their payments electronically.

Conclusion

In many ways the retirement world facing Baby Boomers is very different from the one faced by their parents and grandparents. The days of the gold watch, the firm handshake, and a guaranteed lifetime income stream are becoming a thing of the past. In large measure, responsibility for ensuring a secure, comfortable retirement has been shifted away from the employer and onto the individual. And the burden is that much greater because life expectancy is increasing, and Boomers are likely to find themselves spending more time in retirement than their parents and grandparents ever did.

However, one piece of the retirement picture that has not changed for Boomers is the important role of Social Security. For more than 76 years now, Social Security has provided a solid foundation of income protection that people can count on as they move into retirement. But while it is important for Boomers to understand what the program provides, it is equally important that they understand what it doesn't provide. Yes, Social Security does offer a base of income protection, but Social Security benefits were never intended to be someone's sole source of income, and Boomers need to recognize that fact and plan accordingly. Only then are they likely to experience the same type of comfortable retirement enjoyed by so many of their parents and grandparents.

Common Social Security Myths

If you haven't earned 40 Social Security "credits," you can never collect a Social Security benefit.
FALSE: Even if you haven't earned 40 "credits," it may still be possible to collect a benefit based on the work and earnings of your spouse.

Social Security's Full Retirement Age (FRA) is 66 for everyone.
FALSE: FRA is age 66 for anyone born between 1943 and 1954, but it gradually increases for people born after that.

If you begin to collect a benefit before you have reached your Full Retirement Age (FRA), your monthly payment is permanently reduced.
TRUE: It is roughly a half percent less for each month prior to your FRA that you collect a payment.

Your monthly benefit is increased for each month past FRA that you don't collect a payment.
TRUE: Currently your benefit is increased by two thirds of a percent per month for each month you don't collect, but these Delayed Retirement Credits (DRCs) only accrue until age 70.

Social Security calculates your benefit based on your last three years of work.
FALSE: Benefits are figured using your highest 35 years of earnings under Social Security.

A divorced spouse can collect on his/her ex's work record as long as the marriage lasted at least 5 years.
FALSE: The marriage must have lasted at least 10 years before a divorced spouse can collect. Other conditions must be met, as well.

Once you reach your FRA, you can earn as much as you like without any reduction in your monthly payment.

TRUE: And this applies even if you started collecting Social Security prior to FRA.

You never have to pay federal income tax on the Social Security benefits you receive.

FALSE: Since 1983, Social Security benefits have been subject to federal income tax if your income exceeds a certain threshold.

Social Security benefits automatically go up each year based on the increase in the Consumer Price Index for Urban Wage Earners and Clerical Workers (CPI-W).

TRUE: In determining the exact Cost of Living Adjustment (COLA), Social Security compares the average CPI-W in the third quarter of one year to the third quarter of the following year.

Social Security benefits are always paid on the third of the month.

FALSE: Payments are currently spread throughout the month, based on the recipient's date of birth.

About the Author

Kurt Czarnowski is currently the principal in "Czarnowski Consulting," a retirement planning company that provides "Expert Answers to Your Social Security Questions" (www.CzarnowskiConsulting.com).

Czarnowski is the former Regional Communications Director for the Social Security Administration (SSA) in New England, a position he held from December 1991 until his retirement at the end of 2010. He began his career with SSA in 1976, and during his 34 years with the agency he worked in several different management and staff positions in the Boston area.

As Regional Communications Director, Czarnowski was responsible for coordinating the Social Security Administration's public affairs/public information activities in the six New England states. In this role, he was a frequent speaker at local and regional events for members of the public, and in 2010, he was the featured presenter on "Social Security: Your Retirement Planning Questions Answered," the Social Security Administration's national webinar for financial service professionals: http://www.socialsecurity.gov/webinars/webinarneedtoknow.htm

He is also a regular discussant of Social Security issues on the "Financial Exchange" with Barry Armstrong on WRKO AM 680 in Boston.

In March 2011, he joined the Board of Directors of the Massachusetts Association of Older Americans (MAOA) and was recently elected Vice President. He also serves on the Massachusetts Money Management Project's statewide Advisory Council, and has just become a member of the New England Pension Assistance Project's Advisory Board.

A native New Englander, Czarnowski received a bachelor's degree in history from Hamilton College in Clinton, New York, and a master's degree in public administration from Northeastern University.

He currently lives in Norfolk, Massachusetts with his wife, Anne.

PART II

EMOTIONAL
SECRETS

A successful retirement is so much more than just having enough money. People's expectations have changed. For many people, retirement is no longer just traveling and playing golf. And retirements often last much longer than they did in the past. There are both opportunities and stresses that come with these increased options. Like other people, you may have questions. For example, how will you best manage your time? What is most meaningful to you? How will you deal with the clutter you have accumulated over the years — both emotional and physical? Now that you are home and spending more time with your spouse, how will you manage that relationship during this next phase of your life?

In this section, we'll address some of these issues with the objective of guiding you toward a truly fulfilling retirement.

CHAPTER 3:

RETIREMENT CONVERSATIONS FOR COUPLES

Roberta K. Taylor, RNCS, M.Ed., & Dorian Mintzer, M.S.W., Ph.D.

Introduction

We are in the midst of a longevity revolution. Seventy-eight million "Baby Boomers" and many more on the older fringe are pioneering a new life stage characterized by living and working longer, developing encore careers, and taking advantage of opportunities for growth in their second half of life. With the traditional notion of the "golden years" becoming a thing of the past, retirement is being redefined. Instead of just thinking about what we are retiring from, we need to focus on what we want to retire to.

Many people today are continuing to work for financial reasons. Others enjoy a sense of meaning that comes from purposeful work. Seeking more balance in our lives involves finding ways to integrate work into life rather than life into work.

Although retirement transition is difficult for some people, transitioning to "what's next" can be even more complex for couples. Many couples reach midlife and find that they no longer share the same dreams, goals, and priorities: One partner may want to retire and join the Peace Corps, while the other envisions working for the next five years or starting a small business. Even when couples do agree on what's important and share the same goals and priorities, deciding when and how to retire or where to live and how to manage resources can be challenging. At the same time they may be dealing with changing roles, family issues, relationships, or health care needs, all of which can add stress to their relationship.

How can couples satisfy individual needs and goals and continue to grow and redefine themselves and their relationship as they transition to the next part of life together? This can be a confusing, overwhelming, and scary time in a marriage, but it can also be an opportunity for creating a fulfilling "shared vision" for the future. Beginning to talk about the "10 must-have retirement conversations" well in advance will help to avoid "surprises" as changes become inevitable.

The 10 Must-Have Retirement Conversations

The following 10 conversations came out of research and clinical work. They are the outcomes of several focus groups for couples either approaching retirement or already retired.

1. The timing of retirement
2. Managing finances
3. Changing roles and identity
4. Time together, time apart
5. Intimacy and sexuality
6. Family relationships
7. Health and wellness
8. Lifestyle and where to live
9. Social life, friends, and community
10. Purpose, meaning, and giving back

Have you and your partner had any of these conversations? This simple quiz will help you get a quick glimpse into how each of you views your communication. Remember, this is meant to be a helpful tool for opening up communication. It's not a measure of your relationship.

RETIREMENT CONVERSATION QUIZ

Instructions: Put a T after any of the statements below you believe are true. Do the quiz separately, and then share your results. Notice the areas that you may want to discuss with your partner.

1. We have talked about our timetable for retirement.
2. We make financial decisions together.
3. We know that our roles may change as we go through transition.
4. Having time together and time apart is important to both of us.
5. Intimacy and affection are an important part of our relationship.
6. We agree on our obligations and responsibilities to family.
7. We have planned for future medical and health care needs.
8. We talk about lifestyle and where we may want to live.
9. Social and community connections are a satisfying part of our lives.
10. We share values and know what's important to each other.

How many T's do you have in common? You may want to start the conversation with a topic you already have some agreement around, rather than tackling a highly charged issue.

Getting to "Yes" Together

Obstacles to good communication include gender differences, cultural or societal expectations, relationship issues, personality differences, and family dynamics. When we're not in agreement with our partner, we tend to react rather than respond. With so many potential barriers, it's a wonder that couples find ways to talk together at all!

Good communication is the key to a strong, healthy relationship. Understanding the similarities and differences in how you and your partner process information, approach problems, and make decisions can do a lot to foster good communication.

Relationship patterns tend to develop over time. Sometimes we have the same conversations in the same old way, and feel frustrated and disappointed when we get the same outcome. If this sounds familiar, perhaps it's time to try a different way of communicating.

Communication Tips for Couples

Are you ready to start a conversation with your partner, but don't know how to begin? One of the best ways to engage your partner is letting them know how you feel about an issue and asking for help in working toward a solution. This opens the space for joint problem-solving and minimizes defensive reactions.

1. Start the Conversation

To begin a conversation, you and your partner should:

- Agree to a time and place to talk.
- Set a time frame for the conversation.
- Start with an agreed-upon topic.
- Agree to avoid blaming or shaming .
- Use "I" statements (rather than "you").
- Agree to not bring up past issues.

- Agree to disagree.

Remember, it's not about who's right or wrong—it's about being heard and understood.

2. Be an Active Listener

Show your partner that you want to hear what they are saying.

- Stay present; keep the focus on what your partner is saying rather than on your next response.
- Make eye contact.
- Don't interrupt.
- Don't make assumptions.
- Be aware of nonverbal cues to how your partner may be feeling.
- Notice your own feelings as you listen.
- Avoid being judgmental or defensive.

3. Be Open to Compromise

Knowing how to compromise is an important communication skill. Compromise is not about "right vs. wrong" or "win vs. lose." Instead of being polarized in a struggle, it's possible to achieve a "win-win" solution when you're both willing to make concessions for the good of the relationship. When trying to reach a compromise:

- Approach the conversation with the attitude that agreement is possible.
- Be clear about what is most important to you and why.
- Recognize that you may have different points of view—compromise is not about "right" or "wrong."
- Listen to what is important to your partner.

- If you are disagreeing, don't shut down and dig your heels in; stay open to possibility.
- Look for "win-win" solutions that work for both of you.

Compromises often need to be negotiated, with offers and concessions going back and forth, until you meet somewhere in the middle. It's helpful to determine how important an issue really is to each of you.

A simple way to determine the importance of a given issue is to use a scale of one to ten. For example, on a scale of one to ten, how important is it for you to live near the city? How would the level of importance change if you lived near public transportation and could easily get into the city? Your perspective may change when you and your partner talk together and consider possibilities that allow for compromise.

A word of caution: Making concessions or compromising just to appease your partner can lead to anger and resentment down the road.

4. Suggestions for Problem Solving Together

Creative problem-solving can be an opportunity for growth and shared responsibility. It's a way for couples to work together as a team to achieve positive outcomes. Here are a few tips:

- Make a list of the areas that are most important to you individually.
- Take turns sharing one item at a time (help your partner understand what's important to you and why).
- Don't waste time and energy on things you can't control. Focus on what you can control.
- Make a list of the similarities and differences between your individual lists. Can you find a way to resolve the differences?

- Talk through the pros and cons together. Even if you don't see eye to eye, you will have a chance to hear the other's point of view.
- Start with an issue you agree on. Spend time brainstorming ways you can work together to accomplish a mutual goal. What are one or two action steps to move you toward that goal?
- Continue with other issues, brainstorming each time. Come up with one or two action steps for each issue.

Remember that problem-solving together is a way to share responsibility. If you get stuck, consider working with a therapist or coach to help you get through the obstacles. When couples can talk together without blaming and without being reactive and defensive, chances are their conversations will result in more positive outcomes and a more satisfying relationship.

The Conversations

1. The Timing of Retirement

Some couples are "out of sync" when it comes to timing their retirements. For instance, many women today have entered or re-entered the work force later in life. They may be just "revving up" at the same time their partners are "winding down." There may also be differences in age, health, energy level, income, health care benefits, and job satisfaction. Talking together about individual needs, goals, hopes, and dreams is important when planning for the future.

Although financial considerations are often the "bottom line" when you are trying to decide when to retire, money is not the only factor. As responsibilities and roles change, other pieces of your retirement puzzle become important in mid- to later life. What you need and want in your fifties, sixties, or seventies may be different from what you wanted earlier in life.

There are many variables to your unique retirement transition puzzle, and there are no simple solutions. Talking together and being flexible and open to possibilities can help you discover options you might not have otherwise considered.

2. Managing Finances

Talking about money is often difficult and can be a major stressor in relationships. Understanding your feelings about money and dealing with the "facts" and realities of your unique situation can lead to productive conversations as you plan for your future.

Good decision-making starts with honest and open communication, as well as listening to each other and having the flexibility and courage to let go of how you think things "should be" in order to open up to creative solutions. Being able to talk together about money can be freeing. It can lead to generating options, reducing some of your financial anxieties and fears, and helping you feel more emotionally connected.

Although money is a tool for accomplishing hopes and dreams, it can symbolically represent self-worth, security, freedom, love, power, or control—issues that go way beyond mere dollars and cents. We have all heard it said that "money does not buy happiness," but the fact is that it can provide things that help us enjoy life. The question is often, "How much is enough?" The answer is "It depends." We all have different tipping points when it comes to money, which can become a huge issue for couples when they are trying to decide if and when they can afford to retire. Issues about money are usually deeply rooted. It is not just about how much you have in the bank, but more often about your tolerance for discomfort and risk.

It's normal for money issues to stir up intense feelings and cloud objectivity. But when you're considering a life-changing decision like retiring, you want to be as clear as possible and have all of the facts and information necessary to support your decisions. Working with a knowledgeable and trusted financial advisor can be enormously helpful. A financial advisor can provide information, support, and resources to help you plan in advance and make decisions so that you don't end up outliving your money.

3. Changing Roles and Identity

One of the gifts of reaching the second half of life is being able to reflect on how you have become the person you are and how you can continue to grow in the next chapter of your life. But that means "letting go" in order to open the space for "what's next." This can involve grieving the loss of "what was" and having the courage and motivation to ask "Who am I, now that I'm no longer who I used to be?" When one or both partners are going through transition, the relationship may also need to be redefined as former patterns, roles, and expectations change.

Max was forced to retire from his 40-year career as a cardiac surgeon due to severe arthritis. For several months he spent his time sleeping late, hanging around the house, and watching TV. His wife Barbara, a magazine editor still working long hours, became concerned, as Max seemed depressed and withdrawn.

Max was grieving the loss of his "identity" as a prominent surgeon. His entire life had been focused around his work, and he no longer knew "who" he was or what he was supposed to be doing. Redefining himself and finding a renewed sense of purpose would be a challenge as well as an opportunity.

What happens if you view your retirement transition as an opportunity for transformation, but your partner wants to retire in a more traditional way? On one hand you don't want your partner to feel abandoned, but on the other you want to follow your heart.

A lot depends on how well you communicate with each other. If you are going full speed ahead toward a new endeavor and your partner is feeling left in the dust, it's important to find a way to talk about it. Recognizing that you are in a life stage transition can help to put things in perspective.

All too often the impact of retirement transition is underestimated. What people focus on is the "retirement," but what they are experiencing is a transition that goes beyond the last day of work. And when couples are going through changes that affect their roles and responsibilities, how things are done is up for renegotiation too. Maybe you'd like your partner to take more responsibility for managing the finances, household chores, or social calendar. Couples need to work through these issues so that resentment and anger don't build up.

The process of changing roles and identities in midlife and beyond retirement transition is complex. Although couples are in it together, at times it can feel like a solitary journey, especially when you're trying to reinvent yourself and your relationship.

As we age, we have the opportunity to grow whole, integrating parts that may have been rejected, neglected, or left behind for any number of reasons. The bonus years can be a time of redefinition, but also can be a challenging time for couples as roles and identities shift. Ideally, we grow in wisdom and experience.

4. Time Together, Time Apart

When time patterns begin to shift, paying attention to your relationship balance is important. Open and honest communication is particularly important when you are creating new pathways to the future and finding new ways to nurture your relationship.

Sara and Jim had been married for forty years. Their close relationship, the envy of many friends, was a balance of time spent together and apart. Jim worked in an office and traveled abroad at least once a month. Sara worked at home three days a week. The structure of their work schedules helped them maintain a time balance together and apart, and this added to the success of their marriage. When Jim told Sara that he was thinking about starting a small business and working from home when he retired, she became anxious and worried about how this would affect their relationship. Dealing with time together and apart is a dynamic, ongoing process of being open to what you both need and how things change over time.

Healthy relationships usually have a balance of time together and time apart, which recognizes individuality and independence as well as mutuality and togetherness. Finding the "right" balance can be challenging in retirement transition, especially if one partner wants more time together and the other needs more space. Many couples make assumptions and develop expectations about time together and time apart without talking about it. Making assumptions without checking out what your partner is thinking or feeling can be a setup for disappointment. Dealing with these expectations is a dynamic, ongoing process which necessitates being open to what you both need.

5. Intimacy and Sexuality

Intimacy and sexuality involves the interplay of body, mind, and spirit. The paradox of intimacy and aging is that although sexual desire may decrease or even feel non-existent for some, as we get older the potential for greater intimacy and satisfaction can deepen. Intimacy can fuel the heart and soul of a relationship. Being able to talk about the most intimate parts of your relationship with love and respect can lead to a deeper connection and often a more satisfying sexual relationship.

As time goes by and children leave home, there is often more time, space, and privacy for intimacy. Studies have shown that many adults enjoy sex more as they age. Emotional maturity, a renewed sense of freedom, less inhibition, decreased time pressure, and freedom from earlier responsibilities seem to have a positive effect on the sexual lives of older adults. Couples report having more fun, and enjoying giving and receiving pleasure in many ways. As we age, lovemaking can feel more relaxed and mutual, reflecting emotional closeness as well as physical satisfaction.

Whether or not you continue to have sexual intercourse as you age, the need for intimacy, warmth, sharing, and feeling loved are ageless. Taking comfort in the familiar, accepting yourself and your partner, and finally being able to let go of issues and concerns about body image can be an enormous relief and open the space for greater intimacy. Beginning a new relationship in the second half of life can be a challenge and an opportunity for love, intimacy, and companionship. We enjoy stories of high school sweethearts reconnecting after many years, couples who meet and fall in love after a chance encounter or who perhaps develop a relationship after meeting over the Internet. Whether you're within an existing partnership or entering a new one, the possibilities for love and intimacy in midlife or later abound.

6. Family Relationships

What is your responsibility to your adult children and grandchildren? What if someone you love needs a place to live? What if your elderly parents become ill and need care? Family relationships can be complicated, and you and your partner may not agree on where your obligations begin and end. Being clear about your own feelings and knowing where your partner stands is a good place to start the conversation. In a society with cultural, ethnic, and religious intermarriage, you and your partner may bring different sets of beliefs, values, and family responsibilities to your relationship. In addition, family demographics are changing, and you may be in a first, second, or third marriage, or a long-term relationship without marriage. It can be complicated—to say the least.

Although there are many issues when it comes to families, two prevalent issues today are "boomerang children" (adult children who for one reason or another move back home), and the care of elderly parents.

The return of adult children can be stressful. The stress may be due to financial and privacy-related reasons. You may have already downsized or converted their bedroom into an office or study. What are your responsibilities to adult children who aren't able to live on their own? If you do have an adult child moving in, expectations need to be clear. How will they contribute to the household? What about chores and responsibilities? For how long will they be there? If you want to have a relationship with your adult child after they move out, try to have the conversation before they move in. It's a different conversation if things begin to fall apart.

Making decisions about how to care for an elderly parent, on the other hand, can be heart-wrenching, stressful, and expensive. Whether or not to consider placement or care for a parent at home should be a well thought-out decision made prior to taking action. Although we cannot predict the future, we do know that our parents are aging and will eventually need care. Care-giving can be overwhelming and exhausting, and bring up underlying family issues and old resentments. The stress is cumulative, and without adequate support, can lead to physical and emotional burnout. No matter how devoted you are, you cannot do it alone. The same is true if you end up as a caregiver for your partner. It can be difficult to care for the person you love when you also need to be taking care of yourself.

Family relationships are incredibly complex. The bottom line is that we all basically want the same thing: to be loved, respected, and cared about, and to be part of a family. Since we all want the same thing you would think it would be easy, but of course it's not. We often don't know how to get what we most want. In one way or another, we may find ourselves dealing with past family issues that we bring to our relationships unknowingly.

7. Health and Wellness

How you take care of yourself throughout life will have an enormous impact on your health and wellness now, as well as in the years to come. Most of us want to age well, but we don't always have the resources or know how to do that.

As we get older, some of our parts wear down; we feel an ache here, a pain there, or maybe something that just doesn't seem to be working well. Regular physical exams are a must, and if your body is telling you that something's not right, listen to it and be sure to see your doctor.

In addition to taking care of our physical body, we also need to take care of our brain as well as our emotional and spiritual self. Research has shown that exercising the brain is as important as physical exercise.

We also need to pay attention to practical issues in the second half of life. There are documents that are important to put in place: wills, trusts, powers of attorney, health care proxies, living wills, and so on. Although the tendency is to avoid these issues, it's not a good idea to put them off. The best time to talk about end-of-life issues is when you are healthy and have some distance from them. You don't need to make decisions that are irrevocable, but you do need to start the conversation. It actually may help you feel empowered and freed up, since it's a way to take care of yourself and your survivors.

A positive attitude involves acceptance of the fact that aging is a natural process. Making good choices for our physical and emotional health is crucial. And the truth is that no matter how often we exercise, or how many body parts are repaired or replaced, or how much we spend on special vitamins that promise longevity, how well we eat, or how much cosmetic surgery we have, we are still going to get old and eventually die. All we can do is take good care of ourselves and feel vital for as long as possible — hopefully to our last breath. There are many important decisions that need to be made along the way, and the ones you make today will have a ripple effect tomorrow. Ultimately, aging well is about growing whole rather than growing old.

8. Lifestyle and Where to Live

Retirement transition can be a time of living out dreams, starting your "to-do" list, developing a new vision together, or just staying put. There are many things to consider before decisions are made. Choosing where and how to live is not a one-time conversation. Whatever you decide together, though not irrevocable, puts a process with many ramifications in motion. The more thorough and well-informed you are, the more you'll be able to talk together about the pros and cons of your options. It's an ongoing process that requires flexibility and the ability to adapt to change. Many couples discover that there is nothing stopping them from living their dream. Others may find that either finances or health present obstacles. Although the dream may have to be altered, there are usually ways to have some of what you really want in your life.

The decision of where to live is usually based on lifestyle choices, geographical preferences, proximity to family and friends, health issues and needs — and, of course, financial considerations. You may be wondering why it is important to think about this when you're not ready to retire. It's true that what you want or need at your current age may change as the years pass, but it is better to explore options ahead of time rather than waiting until you are feeling pressured to make a decision.

We go through many changes in life, and often what we wanted in our thirties or forties no longer fits our vision for the life we want to live now. When couples talk together, they may discover things they never knew before. What if your partner's dream is to work on a dude ranch in Montana? Or maybe the dream is selling most of your belongings and building a log cabin in Vermont, or traveling around the country in an RV. Will you be "on board," or do you have dreams of your own? There are many options today worth exploring. Deciding what's right for you will probably take some research and many conversations.

9. Social Life, Friends, and Community

Who are the friends you have known the longest? The ones who knew you "back when?" The ones who hold your secrets? Old friends have a different perspective than those you meet in later years, those who may know your history but didn't live through it with you. Old friends, new friends, acquaintances, and community are all part of your "village" and bring a sense of belonging to your life. There is almost nothing better than having a sense of belonging and connection with like-minded people who know and care about you. It is one of the reasons that people bond around common beliefs or a mission, and join community groups, religious and spiritual organizations, and special interest groups.

We all need a village to sustain involvement and vitality. Even if you have a wonderful partner, no one can or should be expected to meet all of your needs and desires. Finding your "place" and developing friendships, relationships, and community are critically important for continued growth and connection.

As we age, we often have the desire to reach out and give back, to find a balance that enables us to both savor and save the world. Family is one way we seek connection and meaning in life. Having friendships and being involved with community are other ways.

We can be intentional in our choices and use our energy productively for the betterment of family, community, and the planet.

As individuals and as a couple, investing in activities that you enjoy with each other or with friends can enrich and bring meaning to your life. The older you get, the more important it is to create community, especially if work no longer serves that purpose. Isolation can be dangerous to your health, but may be easy to fall into when the familiar structure of day-to-day life is gone and there is nothing to replace it. The opportunities for continued learning and growth, as well as meeting people and having fun, are available—you just need to find them. That might mean taking a risk or stepping out of your comfort zone by doing something that you never thought you could do. It is well worth it to feel that you are engaged in life and part of a community where you are giving as well as receiving.

Participating in community activities can also be a way for the two of you to develop new friendships based on shared interests. When you share interests and activities, not only are you spending time together and expanding your social network, you are also making an investment in your relationship, which fosters a sense of togetherness.

There is no "right way" to develop friendships and support systems. As we age, there are a variety of ways to expand our social network—through hobbies, religious affiliations, courses, volunteer work, or encore careers, or through the Internet and social networks. Some couples enjoy venturing out and learning new things, and others stick with old standbys. Either way, you have to be out there to develop new relationships; they don't usually come knocking at your door.

10. Purpose, Meaning, and Giving Back: What's It All About?

It is not uncommon to reach midlife and wonder, "What's it all about?" After so many years of "doing" and working hard to achieve goals, midlife can feel like an ending, with all of the important parts in the past and nothing to look forward to. At this point we may begin to search for something deeper, something to help us find meaning in life. Although most people look outside of themselves, one of the best ways to find meaning is to look inside. All too often, we spend our lives searching for answers we already have.

Talking with your partner about what is really important in life and how you want to be remembered can deepen and enrich your relationship. You may be able to help each other see how you can make a difference in the world. Couples sometimes begin to consider volunteering, civic engagement, entrepreneurial projects, or involvement with a greater cause. Sharing what is most important and how you want to live the next part of life is an opportunity to begin talking about your legacy.

Both religion and spirituality may play an important role in the second half of life, as we are faced with questions of meaning and mortality. Having a belief in something greater than oneself is comforting, and can provide a sense of belonging to a larger group or community. Research tells us that people who are grounded in such a belief are happier, healthier, and often better able to cope with difficult life circumstances. It is not uncommon for older adults to return to religion or begin to explore spirituality as a way of understanding and bringing meaning to their lives. It may be going to a place of worship, singing in the choir, beginning a meditation or yoga practice, or spending more time in nature. Whatever route you choose, it is probably something that brings you back to yourself and helps you connect with something greater.

The terms "purpose, meaning, and giving back" ultimately relate to how we want to make a difference in the lives of others. It is really about being who you are and sharing your unique talents and gifts. You may question if and how you have made a difference, or think that making a difference means giving something tangible. How you make a difference is in the everyday "gifts," shared in small ways that can be seen in the patterns of your life: the choices you have made, how you've coped with life's challenges, the many ways you have helped and supported others. Whether your contribution is large or small, whenever you make a difference in the lives of others, you are living your purpose.

The word "legacy" usually brings to mind an inheritance of money, property, or family heirlooms. But a legacy is not always tangible, and it is not necessarily about the future. Leaving a legacy can be about living your life so that each day is an opportunity to make a lasting difference.

Our footprints are left in "the sands of time" through work, relationships, contribution, and service. In ways big and small, we all have an impact. The question "What's it all about?" can be a wonderful opening for understanding how we have made a difference and how to make more intentional choices in life. It is never too late to leave a lasting legacy. As individuals and as couples, we can choose to share the gifts of our life with those we love. Whether it is leaving a big endowment, being a meaningful presence in the lives of grandchildren, or volunteering in a hospice program, we can each make a difference in someone else's life. Giving to one means giving to many.

Conclusion

Creating your vision for the future is based on being able to successfully communicate and make decisions together. Because life can be unpredictable, the best plan is a balance of optimism and realism. Retirement isn't a destination — it's a journey. Enjoy the places you visit along the way.

Questions for Retirement Conversations for Couples

The following questions are meant to encourage discussion about various aspects of your retirement transition. After thinking about your responses individually, share them with your partner using the tips in the "Getting to Yes Together" section of the chapter.

- What does the word "retirement" mean to you?
- How will finances influence the decisions you make for your future?
- What can you do to improve communication with your partner?
- What do you wish your partner would do to improve communication?
- What do you most appreciate about your partner?
- What are your expectations for time together and time apart?
- What do you enjoy about your intimate relationships?
- In what ways do family relationships and obligations impact your relationship?
- What do you need to do to prepare for your current and/or future health and wellness needs?
- What criteria are important regarding where and how to live?
- How can you create community around you?
- How do you want to be remembered?

Learn more about these conversations and how couples have resolved some of the issues in *The Couples Retirement Puzzle: 10 Must-Have Conversations for Transitioning to the Second Half of Life* by Roberta Taylor and Dorian Mintzer, available on Amazon, Barnes and Noble, and www.couplesretirementpuzzle.com. Contact us at info@couplesretiremenentpuzzle.com

About the Authors

Roberta Taylor, RNCS, M.Ed., Board Certified Coach and Certified Senior Advisor, is an experienced psychotherapist, retirement transition coach, consultant, author, and speaker. Her career spans almost forty years in both the public and private sector. Her mid-life transition led to the development of her coaching business, Pathmaking for Life, and working with individuals and couples 55 and older who are planning for "what's next." Roberta is passionate about helping her clients successfully navigate retirement transition, develop their vision, and create a fulfilling next chapter of life. Roberta is on the board of the New England Chapter of the National Speakers Association. She is a member of The Life Planning Network, American Society on Aging, International Women's Writing Guild, Toastmasters International, and Wellesley Women in Business. She delivers seminars and facilitates workshops related to retirement transition for professional, educational, and community organizations. She works with financial professionals to bring Holistic Life Planning to their organizations and clients.

Roberta and Dorian Mintzer co-authored *The Couple's Retirement Puzzle: 10 Must-Have Conversations for Transitioning to the Second Half of Life*. Learn more about Roberta at www.pathmaking.com and www.couples-retirementpuzzle.com or you can reach her at rkt@pathmaking.com.

Dorian Mintzer, M.S.W., Ph.D., Board Certified Coach, is a licensed psychologist, life and retirement transition coach, relationship coach, executive coach, consultant, teacher, author, and speaker. She is a Licensed Third Age coach, a 2Young2Retire certified facilitator, and a Licensed Life Change Artist. She is a member of a number of professional organizations such as the National Speakers Association, The Life Planning Network, The American Society on Aging, The International Coach Federation, and The Boston Club for Professional and Executive Women. She facilitates workshops and speaks to community, corporate, and professional groups. Her topics relate to retirement planning for financial planners and other professionals, and mid-life transition and retirement planning issues for individuals and couples.

Mintzer is founder of the "Boomers and Beyond Special Interest Group" for interdisciplinary professionals, and a new series: "Revolutionize Your Retirement: Interviews with Experts to help You Create a Fulfilling Second Half of Life." She combines her life experiences and expertise in adult development, positive psychology, and holistic life planning in her work with helping individuals and couples navigate the second half of life. She also teaches in the Gerontology Certificate Program at Regis College in Weston, MA.

She is co-author with Roberta Taylor of *The Couple's Retirement Puzzle: 10 Must-Have Conversations for Transitioning to the Second Half of Life*. She is a contributing author to *65 Things to do When You Retire, Remarkable and Real*, and *Making Marriage a Success*. You can learn more about Dori at www.revolutionizeretirement.com and www.couplesretirementpuzzle.com or reach her at dorian@dorianmintzer.com.

CHAPTER 4:

HOW TO BE YOUR BEST FROM THE INSIDE OUT, EVEN AFTER 50

Sallie Felton

Where has the time gone? Our youth seems just a blip on the radar screen, followed by the responsibility of maturity with all its different routes! Are you staring down the barrel of retirement or planning for it? Is it causing you mental and emotional "clutter" and perhaps even anguish? Do you hear yourself asking:

- "Where will we/I live?"
- "Are we/I moving?"
- "What are we/I going to do?"
- "Where will we/I go?"
- "We/I are fearful of this next step in our lives…this change."
- "We/I thought this would be a lot easier."

We tend to think life gets easier after 50, or that the second half of our life has fewer priorities than before. However, for some life actually gets more complicated. Dealing with adult children, divorce, grandparenting, aging parents, our own physical health, finances, and just thinking about retirement can be stressful in its own right. Let's face it; we all have clutter to some degree or another, and the older we get, some of us hold onto it longer than others. By peeling off the physical and the emotional clutter like the leaves of an artichoke, we get to the center...*the heart.*

The age of 50 and beyond should be a time of wisdom, coming into our true center, living a time of reflection. In order to be our best from the inside out, we need to begin to "de-clutter." But how?

Clutter comes in three forms: physical, emotional, and mental.

Physical clutter is easy to see. It's the piles of paper on the counter tops, the guest room that houses unused furniture, and the 30-odd years of accumulated "stuff" throughout the house, breeding in the basement and the attic.

Mental clutter is the constant "to-do list" that becomes a 24/7 running tape in our mind. It's a list that is added to daily, never ending, leaving us feeling frustrated, exhausted, and worried.

Emotional clutter comes from the heart. It's made up of those unresolved, non-discussed feelings we all have, and it can cause worry, resentment, anger, bitterness, envy, and judgment, just to name a few.

Throughout this chapter, we'll talk about how you can reduce, reuse, and recycle to downsize your life to be the best from the inside out.

The future is something which everyone reaches at the rate of 60 minutes an hour, whatever he does, whoever he is."
—*C. S. Lewis*

Moving and Downsizing the Physical Clutter fo[r] Retirement

Many people downsize for retirement. You may be beginning [to] ask yourself, "What can we pare down?" "What is not servicing u[s] any longer?" "Times have changed; what can we let go of now?"

If you're like us, you've lived in the same house for the last 30-plus years and have decades of "stuff" to sort through. Some items may be hidden far back in the closets, under the eaves, or deep in the basement. You may consider moving to a townhome development, apartment building, or condo complex which provides all the amenities: lawn service, trash pickup, home maintenance, etc. This can ease the physical pressure on you as you get older. Or it could be you wish to be nearer to other people.

Did you know that besides divorce, death, and loss of a job, moving is ranked up there as one of the top stressors? To help make this process less stressful, I am going to show you how you can begin by de-cluttering your physical possessions. First, you should be clear about why you are moving to this new location:

- To be closer to your family?
- To be in a warmer climate?
- To be in a less expensive area/state?
- To be closer to medical facilities?
- To maintain less property?

If moving to a less expensive area of the country is more feasible for you and your pocketbook, think it through carefully. Consider where your family resides; is there an area in and around them that is not too expensive? Is there a possibility for an in-law apartment? What would that feel like for all involved?

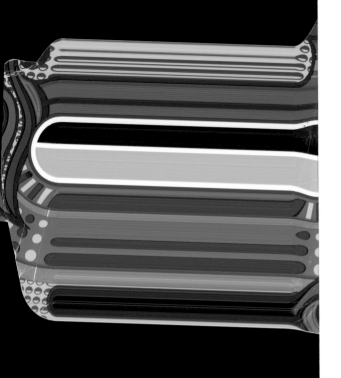

Take Pictures of Your New Environment

- What will you need to take?
- Identify a use for each of the rooms in your new abode.
- Measure each of the rooms.
- How much storage space are you allowed?

Use Professional Organizers/Moving Managers

They can help in the downsizing, especially if this is going to be stressful. Remember, you're still in control of what it is you want to take with you.

What Do You Take?

- Once you have identified which room is what, measure the perimeter of each room, noting where the windows and closets are located.
- Make a list of your favorite pieces of furniture, and *measure the furniture* first to make sure it fits in the designated room/

space. This is critical. You can't take four bedroom sets and expect to fit them into a two-bedroom condo.

- Keep only those items and belongings you will have room for in the smaller space.

Tip: *It was important for my mother to make her new environment similar to the one she was used to. She incorporated an old beam from the dining room ceiling, added corner cabinets, brought her hand-forged trellis for the outside garden, and built extra storage. And more built-ins! She gave the furniture that wouldn't fit to us.*

Before the Move: Choose, Toss, Donate

- Make a list of every room in your existing house/apartment/condo.
- Go room-by-room, focusing on sorting.
- What you'll need: plenty of boxes, garbage bags, felt markers, duct tape, etc.
- Boxes: label the boxes: 1) Keep, 2) Donate to Charity, 2) Give to Family/Relative/Friends, 3) Toss, etc.

Tip: *My mother was pro-active in asking us what furniture we wanted. Then she added a sticker with our initials on it. It gave her great pleasure to know what we cared about, and that made it easier for her to de-clutter. She even asked her grandchildren...our son received the ship's wheel from the minesweeper my father commanded in WWII as his college graduation present! Our daughter received a complete collection of Shakespeare, and another son a piece of furniture. This was a win-win situation for all!*

- When choosing, repeat the three-second rule... "I love it, It's useful, or Out it goes" and *decide.*

- To stay on track, sort for no more than an hour or two at the most. We want success here, not exhaustion. Use a kitchen timer or play your favorite CD until it ends to hold yourself accountable.
- Label boxes and remove from the room when they're filled.
- Donate items (sites like freecycle.org or craigslist.com help keep the process from becoming burdensome).
- Charity resources: Big Brothers Big Sisters, Salvation Army, shelters, churches, schools, etc.
- If you have to, put items into storage (for only a short time) if you are unsure what to do with them for now. Make certain boxes are duct taped and labeled. Amazing as it seems, you might find after a few months that you actually don't need those items and you can part with them.

Paper Clutter/Keep or Toss?

Things to Save

The big questions I hear are, "What do I save and what do I toss?" The first thing I say to all is "Talk to your accountant and/or lawyer before throwing out any financial or legal papers." Here is a guide from Barbara Hemphill's *Taming The Paper Tiger*:

1. Automobile records: keep titles, registration, and repairs for as long as you own the vehicle.
2. Appointment books: (past) 1–10 years, according to your comfort level and whether you use them for tax records, references, or memorabilia.
3. ATM slips: maximum 6 years if needed for tax purposes.
4. Bank statement: maximum 6 years if used for tax purposes.
5. Credit card statements: maximum 6 years if tax-related pur-

chases on statements; otherwise until annual interest statement is issued by the company.

6. Catalogs/magazines: until the next issue…then recycle it!
7. Dividend payment records: until annual statement is supplied by company, and just annual statements thereafter.
8. Household inventory and appraisals: as long as current. Take video/pictures of items.
9. Insurance policies: auto, homeowners, liability, as long as statute of limitations in the event of late claims.
10. Insurance policies: disability, medical, life, personal property, umbrella, as long as you own.
11. Investments: purchase records, as long as you own the investments.
12. Investments: sales records, maximum of 6 years for tax purposes.
13. Mortgage or loan discharge: as long as you're paying the loan, or 6 years after discharge.
14. Property bill or purchase: as long as you own the property.
15. Receipts:
    - Appliances: as long as you own them
    - Art, antiques, collectibles: as long as you own them
    - Clothing: for the length of the returns period
    - Credit card slips: until the statement comes in and you can match purchases
    - Furniture: as long as you own the item, in case repair is needed
    - Home improvements: for life of the warranty or longer to track reliability record of service people and their rates
    - Major purchases: life of the item
    - Medical and tax/related: maximum 6 years
    - Rent: your cancelled check is sufficient
    - Utility bills: current bill and one previous year's to check

billing patterns

- Warranties and instructions: life of the warranty or item. Stick a label with warranty expiration date and service repair number on the bottom of the appliance. If something breaks down, you've got an easy way to check if the item is still covered without having to go to your file drawer
- Resume: as long as it's current
- Safe-deposit box key and inventory: as long as it's current
- Tax records, bank statements and canceled checks, certificates of deposit, contracts, charitable contributions, credit statements, income tax returns, lease and loan agreements, loan payment books, pension plan records, pay stubs: current year, plus 6 prior years
- Vital records: adoptions papers, birth and death certificates, citizenship papers, copyright/patents, marriage certificate, divorce decree, letter of "last instructions" to executor or heirs, medical illness and vaccination records, passports, powers of attorney, Social Security record, wills…permanently!

Things to Toss

Get the shredder, recycle to your heart's content…*now it's time to purge*. Here are some suggestions for things that Julie Morgenstern believes you don't need to think twice about:

1. Junk mail
2. Expired coupons
3. Outdated schedules
4. Old greeting cards, unless you want to recycle the parts not written on and use for gift tags
5. Old grocery receipts

6. Invitations to past events
7. Expired warranties and service contracts
8. Instructions for items you no longer own
9. Expired insurance policies
10. Unread magazines
11. Old catalogs, keep only current ONE
12. Investment and banking brochures you never used
13. Cancelled checks, unless needed for tax purposes
14. Checkbooks, if they're more than 6 years old, or the account has been canceled
15. Receipts for non-tax-deductible items
16. Business cards from people whose names you don't recognize
17. Old tourist brochures (I use these for wrapping paper)
18. Old road maps
19. Solicitations from charities you don't intend to give to
20. Recipes you haven't tried in 5 years
21. Bad-quality photos or ones you simply don't like
22. Articles or clippings you haven't reread in more than 5 years

So now that you de-cluttered…how much freer are you feeling?

To Sell or Store?

Okay, you have decided what you are taking with you; now what about those possessions you no longer want? What to do? There are several areas from which to choose to unload your items:

- Garage sale
- Auction
- eBay
- Craigslist, etc.
- Newspaper

Garage sales are a great way to reduce and recycle your possessions with a financial profit in the end. What you think is your "trash" could become someone else's treasure! The benefits are reduced mental clutter, less worries, less to pack, less moving fees, and a bit of profit, to name just a few.

> **Tip:** *Take a picture of all the possessions that don't fit into your new surroundings, but you wish to keep. Email them to your children, family, friends…is there anything they might wish to have? ASK! If no one wants them, don't hold on to these items for sentiment, because they will add to your mental and financial clutter both.*

If you are new to this arena, there are professionals who will take on the task for a percentage of the profits. Look up Professional Organizers or Professional Movers, or call your real estate agent.

> **Tip:** *When both of our parents died, we were in charge of cleaning out their townhouse. It was a monumental, overwhelming and painful task. We broke it down into manageable steps, baby steps…room by room. I was given instructions to find an auctioneer for the few pieces we had left. One never knows the value of some items…a blackened dusty old cane in the back of the closet fetched $10,000! Who knew??? Only when it was appraised did we have a clue as to its value.*

To store or not to store, that is the question! This is a very personal decision. I spoke with one of my clients who was downsizing. She opted to store her unused possessions (thinking her adult children would take them off her hands) for seven years. Her bill in the end was a whopping $48,000! It caught my attention *big time*!

> *Invest the profits from the sale of your old home, if there are any, and draw on the investment account to pay for the rent or a smaller mortgage on your new home. This can ease the pressure on your other retirement accounts and Social Security income, further reducing your sources of worry as time goes on."*
>
> —*John Mack,*
> How to Downsize to Simplify Your Life

Saying Good-Bye

For some individuals this may be easier than for others. Unless you have gone through this experience, make no judgments. The reasons people move are endless.

> **Tip:** *Whatever the reason, give yourself time to say "Good-bye" to your familiar surroundings. Walk around each room, remember the memories, and take it all in. Take pictures if you need to in order to remember a garden, a favorite place, or a particular space.*

> *Start by doing what's necessary, then what's possible, and suddenly you are doing the impossible."*
>
> — *Saint Francis of Assisi*

I'm Not Getting Older, I'm Getting Better

I dislike the humorous cards, jabs, and jokes about age and aging. There was a time when I laughed at them, but not anymore. I've heard too many "seniors" talk about feeling displaced, being rejected by their families, or becoming burdensome. As Ellen Wood puts it in *Think and Grow Young—Powerful Steps to Create a Life of Joy,*

"Society is handicapped by the prevalent ideas and beliefs about what aging looks and feels like, ideas inherited from generations past. We've been taught that growing old is grim, that it's natural to lose many of our aptitudes and abilities and sure isn't fun. Not so many decades ago, we were also taught that man couldn't fly. But there were a few who chose not to accept the impossibility of flight and, instead, figured out how."

- If you look in the mirror and don't like what you see
- If you find yourself saying, "I'm too old to do that," or "I keep forgetting things"
- If your spirit is worn out and you've forgotten how powerful and magnificent you are (or never really knew it)
- If you feel like the best part of your life is behind you…

We don't have to grow old, or become weak, ill, disoriented, and afraid. We can instead choose to grow younger. Ellen Wood and other pioneers, including scientists and physicians, are shaking the roots of the prevailing belief system and discussing instead how we can grow younger as we age.

I met and interviewed Ellen Wood, at that time 75, and she was on a mission to help transform America's elders into empowered, valued members of society. She said, "I am usurping Senior Citizens Day and calling it Amazing Elders Day. What's a senior citizen anyway? Someone who's old enough to collect Social Security, apply for Medicare, and get in the movies for half price."

What is an elder?

"An elder is anyone who feels they've lived long enough to absorb wisdom from the people, situations, and circumstances of their life. An Amazing Elder is someone ready to share their gifts of wisdom with anyone who asks," proclaims Wood.

Amazing wisdom can mean the difference between living a powerful life of joy and blessings, and living with sadness and regrets. I learned much from my Grandmother "Bee": 1) the perfect techniques for pulling molasses candy, 2) darning socks, 3) needlework, 4) polishing silver, and 5) tending perennial gardens.

I learned about the Depression Era and her strong sense of re-use, recycle, repurpose...and *never waste*. I revered her courage in taking her three small children to Europe to live after her husband died of pneumonia at the age of 32. I admired her strength and sense of adventure. How lucky we are if we have an amazing elder in our life and can learn from them!

So how can you feel younger as you get older?

"Once we understand how much thoughts and beliefs determine what takes place in our bodies and in our lives, we can begin to take control, change our thought patterns, replace limiting beliefs, and create the joyful life we want," says Wood.

Here Are Nine Tips to Fill Your Time:

1. BEGIN a daily program of practices by **creating the goal of growing younger.** Ellen Wood did this at 71. She has a clearer, sharper mind and stronger body than ever before, and has regained the energy, stamina, flexibility, and vitality she enjoyed 30 years ago

2. BEGIN by **quieting the spirit**...worry less, breathe more, absorb yourself in beauty...music, reading anything that brightens your soul

3. BEGIN by **being more physical**: walk, stretch, swim, yoga... do what you love

4. BEGIN by **reaching out** to those you love, share your stories, your knowledge

5. BEGIN by **mentoring**, who can you take under your wing; where can you volunteer

6. BEGIN by **exploring** a new "hobby"
7. BEGIN by **taking baby steps** to step out of your comfort zone
8. BEGIN by **changing bad habits**: reduce television watching, try reading instead; if you smoke or drink too much, talk to your doctor to get support and solutions to reduce this, and find more time to spend doing physical activities
9. BEGIN by **removing yourself** from unhealthy relationships and/or add positive relationships to your network

Creating New Habits

You too can learn how to reverse aging! It's a matter of taking control of the process, of making conscious choices and creating new habits. So who are you going to be tomorrow…an elder or *an amazing elder*? It's your choice…be someone daring, be bold and spread your wings; let's grow younger together. Here are a few tips on what you can do for someone:

- If they are recovering from an illness or surgery…bring them a dinner, do an errand, get their mail, bring them flowers or magazines, play cards with them, bring them tea or coffee, do a load of laundry
- Offer to trade services. "Can you help me with x, y, z and I can do … for you"
- Ask to help out planting a new garden or share the weeding of a vegetable garden…you can both reap the benefits
- The ideas are endless…What do you want help with?…*ask away*

> *The older I get, the greater power I seem to have to help the world; I am like a snowball—the further I am rolled, the more I gain."*
>
> *—Susan B. Anthony*

Talk About It!

How many of you have either thought about your own mortality, or are dealing with parents or loved ones? Are you the caregivers or do you know others who are? We all need to realize the fact that we will not live forever, so why not make it easier for the ones we leave behind?

If something were to happen to you, do your loved ones know where to put their hands on all those important papers and documents, such as:

- Health care proxy
- Burial instructions
- Safe deposit
- Safe combination
- Life insurance policy
- Social Security cards
- Homeowners policy
- Child's guardian papers
- Credit card list
- Check book
- Savings deposit book
- Partnership agreements
- Business records
- Deeds
- Will and requests
- Computer user names and passwords (who knew!)

…just to name a few!!

For example: I'm 61 years young, but we had our three grown children put their signatures on our safe deposit card held at the bank. If for any reason something should happen to my husband or me, they'll have full access to the safe deposit box. I learned firsthand that my mother never had any other person's name on her card after my father died; his was the only other name. So one day when we both were in her bank, I asked her who was the other signature... her reply was, "Do I need one?"...we left with *my signature* on the signature safe deposit card. Note: My mother died three weeks later...

So will it be a search and rescue mission? People we love have enough to worry about dealing with grief and despair...there is a simpler way to go. I have revised *Stop the Looking: Location of Important Papers and Documents* (five pages of fill in the blanks) and would be happy to share it with you. Send me your email address and put "Important Papers" in the subject line...I will send you the Word document. Simple as that.

Grieving and Emotional "Clutter"

The death of a parent disturbs our roots and shakes our foundation. I remember in 1999 when my father was diagnosed with emphysema and congestive heart failure, hearing the doctor's words, "Your Dad may have a year or two." I was stunned; numb...this can't be happening. My inner child was screaming, "This is not okay. I am not ready to deal with his death." This was not in the cards, cannot be happening... of course my parents will live forever. *Wrong!*

It's not by surprise that my sisters are my best friends. It wasn't always like that growing up, but we worked at it through the years, confronting each other and working through issues. They would each be by my side and me theirs at a moment's notice, unconditionally. It's because of that bond I believe we were able to rally around, taking turns caring for Dad and later for Mom, who was diagnosed with lung cancer the summer before Dad died in 2000. We joked with our parents that there was a reason they had five daughters… as constant caregivers.

Both of our parents made it very clear there was to be no nursing home in their future, though there are families where that is not an option. All five of us gathered around and came up with options, plans, schedules, and support systems. Some of them our parents thought were overdone, overprotective, and overly committed. However, when I asked, "If you were taking care of me, what would you do?" Bingo! Same solutions.

We spent wonderful days caring for him and later for Mom. Those two years gave me a greater sense of unconditionally "giving" than I ever thought I had in me. I looked at every task—changing Depends, changing a soiled bed, feeding a meal—never as a job or burden but as coming full circle. It was my turn and my privilege to give back to them for all the years they nurtured me. Whenever there was a tense moment, we used humor; we shared stories and memories and soothed each other with touch.

Before Dad died, my sisters asked if I would say something at his funeral. Dad and I were always joined at the hip, so I felt honored. As I visited with him I often wondered what I would say…and then I would begin to write and write some more. The feelings poured out, even our butting heads came onto the pages. Then I did something I instinctually, from a cellular level, *had to do*. I drove down to see him one afternoon and asked if I could share with him what I was going to read at his funeral. He smiled! I sat beside him, holding his hand and began to read. Tears poured from both of us. I got to say what was in my heart.

He knew for years how I felt, but how many times do we really sit down, take the time, and say it…really say it? Of all the people in the world I wanted to hear those words, it was Dad.

So if your foundation has been jostled by the death of a loved one and you haven't had the chance to tell them how much they meant to you, here's something you can do. Take up a journal and begin to write, tell them what he/she meant to you…what you struggled with, issues you wish were resolved. Let it out…grieve…the healing will take place in time. Then ceremoniously burn it outside, letting the Universe deliver it if they are no longer around.

P.S. I put my letter into Dad's pocket before he was cremated. My words will always be with him.

> " One cannot get through life without pain… What we can do is choose how to use the pain life presents to us."
> —Bernie S. Siegel, M.D.

Let's review…in order for this transition in your life to become easier, less cluttered, five things must be done:

1. A person needs to make physical space for it…be it a new interest, activity, or hobby; i.e. make space for what you want to come into your life. If you're going to downsize, it's a new place to live: a condo, a townhouse or a smaller house. What do you think this would do for your inner clutter, your mind? It begins the slow process of de-cluttering from the inside out.

2. One must be open to receiving what the universe has to offer. If you are open to receiving what the universe has to offer, instead of being stressed that you don't have a particular item, realize that you might come across just what you need by finding it in the newspaper or via a friend. Two great sources are www.freecycle.org and www.craigslist.com

3. Create time…create time for yourself in your calendar the same way as you make an appointment in your calendar for the doctor…you are just as important. Mark your appoint-

ment with yourself in your BlackBerry, iPhone, or physical calendar. Make yourself accountable for your appointment.

4. Be your authentic self. Love yourself just as you are, with all the wrinkles, dark circles, crows' feet, and loose skin. There's no need for Botox or lifts. Do what you like to do, nurture your wants and your needs. Be gentle with yourself, either in a relationship or by making space in your house for another person. Is there space in your heart?

    Sometimes there is so much mental clutter that you may not know what you really want in your heart. This is a perfect time to find out what you want. How do you do it?

    Write down in a journal what it is you want to come into your life. Be specific and perfectly clear: what is it that you want, when do you want it, and what does it look like, feel like, or smell like?

5. Now is the time to commit to action. Keep a journal, and every day think of one small step you can take that will lead you to your goal. It only has to take five minutes a day, but you will be that much closer to your goal. *What do you think that would feel like?*

Asking for Help

Why are we tongue-tied when it comes to asking for help? When we were younger it was common for us to ask for help when we needed an extra hand, but as we grew older society told us we needed to become independent.

So how do we change?

When working with my clients, I find that some have a harder time than others in this particular arena. One of them is a single Baby Boomer who finds herself wearing the proverbial armor, complete with the crest "I can do it all" emblazoned on the front. But can she really do it all?

What's she missing? She told me that she really wants to ask for help, but fears that her independence will be tarnished if she does. So I asked her, "What would you gain by asking?" She sat back and pondered this question. With a brighter look in her eye she replied, "I would gain a companion to help me with something I wanted to complete or accomplish. I would be able to finish things I can't do alone." I then asked, "What could you do today to move yourself in that direction?" She said she had a problem with one of her computers and needed to have someone educate her on what to do. We came up with a list of friends/relatives/professionals who could help her. Walking out of the office, she looked back to say, "I will call my nephew…he is so good with all sorts of electronics. And it will be so great to see him after so many months."

So what did my client get? She not only received help from her nephew, but she is rekindling a relationship with him that she misses.

Ask for What You Need

A common assumption is that if I ask for help, I am indebted to the person who helps me. Or even worse….that she/he will resent me for asking for their help. Nope, I don't buy this one at all.

Everyone loves to have the chance to help someone else out. If you can help another person out, jump on it. If you have a hard time asking for help, take baby steps, take the risk, and ask; you will be surprised when your armor becomes more pliable.

Take a deep breath and launch the words right out of your mouth. It doesn't have to be monumental. Be direct, and don't apologize!

You will be amazed at how many people are willing and even eager to lend a hand. Everyone wants to feel they are useful, appreciated, and thought about. So go on, pick up the phone; allow someone to help you out!

Have You Forgotten to Play?

Remember this, Baby Boomers become more "booming" in their later years, but they sometimes find that the best part of them is hidden/silent. I am talking about their relationship to their inner child; the one that lives deep within each of us. It was that child who used to run through the puddles, play outside all night, and do crazy things. What was the craziest thing you've done lately? We all need to play and have fun! It is critical to nurturing ourselves. So drop what you are doing, take off your shoes and socks…wiggle those toes, and try to pick something off the floor with your toes. Are you laughing now? Do something spontaneous.

Just before writing this I had two choices of roads to drive home. I chose the one with the largest puddle…one that covered both sides of my car as I drove through it. I could feel the child inside me giggle. I laughed outwardly and for three seconds I was six years old again, wading through the pond on my inner tube. What will you do?

Conclusion

Life transitions are constant for every person, from birth to death and everywhere in between. It is one's ability to get through them that will define their quality of life. Getting through such changes, and more importantly thriving, can be difficult to do on one's own when faced with new challenges. But it is my hope that releasing the mental, physical, and emotional clutter from your life, you will head smoothly into this new and exciting adventure called retirement.

 *Grow old along with me! The best is yet to be."*
—*Robert Browning*

Questions for Being Your Best From the Inside Out

When thinking about the next half of my life and a possible new living environment, if there are physical items I no longer need, have I been responsible for removing them?

In order to make it simpler for others to locate my important papers, have I been diligent about having all important documents in one place?

In order to make it simpler for others to sign in/log in to my computer, have I been diligent about writing down all my websites, user names, and passwords?

How would I rate myself in relation to my POSITIVE mental attitude of growing older? Does it need some work?

Am I good about asking for help when I need it?

To relieve some of the "emotional clutter" have I had "the end of life/my wishes met" conversation with my family?

As we all age, it is important we find areas of interest/passions; have I found or listed mine?

Resources

Hemphill, Barbara, *Taming The Paper Tiger*, Random House trade; 3rd Rev edition (April 1992).

Morgenstern, Julie, *Time Management From The Inside Out* (An Owl Book, Henry Holt and Company, NY; copyright 2004).

Morgenstern, Julie, *Organizing From The Inside Out* (An Owl Book, Henry Holt And Company, NY; copyright 2004).

"How To Downsize to Simplify Your Life" by John Mack, *eHow* Contributor, August 13, 2011.

Think and Grow Young—Powerful Steps to Create a Life of Joy by Ellen Wood

About the Author

As featured on ABC, NBC, CBS, and FOX News affiliates across the country, **Sallie Felton**, president of Sallie Felton LLC, is a life coach, international radio talk show host, author, facilitator, inspirational speaker, and former hypnotherapist and deep imagery therapist. She was formally trained with MentorCoach LLC and certified as a Professional Certified Coach (PCC) by the International Coach Federation. Drawing on all types of counseling and acting as a partner and cheerleader, it is her passion to help individuals who are either in a transition or trying to seek order and balance in their lives… even those who are totally disorganized…mentally, physically, or emotionally! Her unique approach, which is equal parts honesty, playfulness, and genuine compassion, is what's earned Sallie accolades from clients, colleagues, and radio show guests alike. As she says, "This is a process, so let's start where you stand, right now, right here. What do you want, how will you achieve it, and when are you going to start?"

Sallie excels in facilitating interactive workshops, working with such organizations as The American Heart Association, Mary Kay, hospital groups, corporations, associations, and professional and non-profit organizations.

Sallie's two radio shows, "A Fresh Start" (empowering oneself) and "Light At the End of The Tunnel" (dealing with depression), leave no stones unturned. Asking powerful questions of her world-renowned guests and offering her 525,000 subscribers tips, tools, and "aha" moments to aid them in their own self-discovery are some of her greatest strengths. Heard in 140 countries, her shows are broadcast live in Seattle, WA on 106.9FM Channel HD 3, on ContactTalkRadio.com, and on the WebTalkRadio. net as well as through the World Wide Web.

Co-author of the Ebook/Workbook, "Clutter Free and Clear: How To Take Charge of Your Time and Space" Sallie has co-authored *The Small Business Owner's Assessment Tool* as well as several books, including *Stepping Stones to Success* (2010) with Deepak Chopra, and *GPS for Success* (2011) with Stephen R. Covey. Her most recent Ebook, *Start Where You Stand, Finding Your True North in the Life/Work Balance* (2010) is a "how-to-workbook" on finding one's inner and outer balance in the game of life. In her Amazon #1 best-selling book, *If I'm So Smart Why Can't I Get Rid of This Clutter?* Sallie shares her own private stories of her wins and struggles dealing with the three types of clutter we all have. As she said, "I put myself out there; I wore my heart on my sleeve.

It doesn't get more honest than this."

She and her husband, Conway, live north of Boston, Massachusetts with their mischievous Alaskan malamute, Kodi. They have three adventurous grown children.

PART III

PHYSICAL
SECRETS

We have all heard it, and we know it's true — without your health you have nothing. The plans you've made and the dreams you have can be curtailed or even derailed without a focus on being healthy and staying healthy. In retirement, staying healthy is necessary in order to enjoy the fruits of your years of labor. In addition to staying healthy, there are other physical issues to think about. Where should you reside during this next phase of life? What considerations are important? Mountains and the outdoors? Ocean? Proximity to family? Weather? When we think about physical considerations, it includes looking at the both internal health of your body, and the external environment of your living space.

In this section we present some ideas on how to help you pursue the physical side of life so that you can maximize the journey into retirement.

CHAPTER 5

THE FOUR PILLARS OF HEALTH

Dr. Peter Martone

You make hundreds of choices each and every day. Some of them you are conscious of making, like the decision to read this chapter right now, but others have become so habitual that you no longer even recognize them as choices — like waking up and having that cup of coffee. It's important to recognize these choices.

Every choice you make, be it conscious or unconscious, impacts you and your health in some way. And these choices can either move you closer to a state of optimal health and well-being or move you further away from it. At Atlantis Chiropractic Wellness Centers, we have discovered that people make choices based on their belief system.

Your belief system is what you "believe" to be the right things to do. This system has been engrained in you by the environs and the people surrounding you throughout your life. It's your belief system that motivated you to wake up this morning and drink that cup of coffee, rather than wake up and drink water on the way to the gym. Whatever the action or decision was, it was driven by a belief. You may have grown up hearing that milk "does the body good" and since then, you've been making sure to drink milk every day. Or, conversely, you may have grown up thinking it's normal to smoke cigarettes.

In the United States, our beliefs have led us to rank last on the list of the 50 healthiest countries in the world. We are dead last! If you want to add *life to your years and years to your life*, then please read this with an open mind and start to challenge some of those beliefs that are preventing you from living the life that you deserve.

I want to start by talking about what I believe is the most overlooked system in the human body. It is the master controller of the whole body, but yet we take it for granted every day—your central nervous system (CNS).

Your nervous system is the master control system of your body. It is made up of your brain, spinal cord, and spinal nerves (they come off the spine) called peripheral nerves. Your brain is the power source and control center of literally every function in your body. If it dies, you die. Your brain sends 100% of your body's information and energy down your spinal cord first. No function in the body happens without being controlled by your central nervous system. The CNS regulates everything. If you have a stomach problem, heart problem, sugar problem, or whatever it may be, all of it is being controlled by the CNS. When I talk about improving your quality of life by changing your lifestyle, I always look at how your body has to adapt to the lifestyle stress that you are putting on it.

It is important to define what stress is. Most people think about stress as a negative emotion based on an event. Webster's dictionary, for example, defines stress as a force that causes change. For the purposes of this chapter I am going to redefine it as a force that causes your body to adapt. You can have either eustress or distress.

Eustress is a stress that causes positive change in your body, and distress is a stress that causes negative change in your body.

Regardless of whether they are positive or negative, there are three types of stress your body is constantly adapting to every microsecond: physical, emotional, and biochemical.

Physical:

- Positive physical stress: exercise, good sleeping habits, stretching, etc.
- Negative physical stress: injuries, poor posture, sleeping position, etc.

Biochemical:

- Positive biochemical stress: staying hydrated, eating fruits, eating vegetables, etc.
- Negative biochemical stress: smoking, alcohol consumption, processed food, etc.

Emotional:

- Positive emotional stress: writing a book, reading, goal setting, love, etc.
- Negative emotional stress: work problems, relationship problems, fighting, etc.

When your body adapts to a positive stress, it causes an improvement in your health, and when the body adapts to a negative stress, it causes your health to suffer. You are constantly moving either toward health or away from it, depending on your lifestyle choices. But it's not all black and white—everyone makes both good and bad choices. That's why we talk about our health as being on a health continuum.

Your CNS controls how your body adapts to the stress you put

Figure 4:
The Health Continuum: Which way are you moving?

DEATH

HEALTH

on it. This is where most medical minds go wrong. They do not link the importance of a healthy functioning nervous system to the cause of disease. I am going to give you an example below of how our nervous system regulates our body to adapt to doing a simple task: drinking a glass of milk.

Your body's adaptation to milk

Act 1

When you drink a glass of milk, the milk goes into your stomach and your stomach tells the body to produce acid to break it down. Then when the pH is right, it releases the milk into the lower portion of the digestive tract for digestion. Let's take a look at the first phase of the lower GI tract called your duodenum. This is where calcium and phosphates are absorbed. When food enters the duodenum, it has to pass channels in the lining of the duodenum. There is a gate keeper controlled by the CNS—think of it as similar to a security guard at a gated community. Only certain nutrients can pass through.

In the duodenum, there is a channel that only lets calcium and phosphates through. But the security guard likes phosphates much more than it likes calcium, so when there are more phosphates around, the guard will let them through and keep the calcium back. Milk is very high in phosphates as well as calcium, so as you can imagine this creates a problem. The security guard is only going to let the phosphates in and not the calcium, which means the calcium stays in the GI tract to be excreted by the urine.

Act 2

Now that the phosphates are in the bloodstream (but not the calcium), what's the problem? Well, phosphates are very acidic, which means that the pH of your blood drops when you have high amounts of phosphates in your bloodstream. Acidic blood is corrosive to the lining of your artery walls. So what happens?

When the nervous system tells the brain that there is damage being done to the artery walls, the brain calls upon its acid defense team based in your bones. That defense team is your calcium stores. The brain makes the decision to release the calcium from the bones to protect you from the lifestyle choice that you made and it knows that you will never get more troops back.

The body's adaptation to drinking milk actually results in weakened bones because of the acidic effect of the phosphates!

> **Side Note:** *You cannot rebuild your calcium stores after the age of 35—you just keep losing them. Drinking milk to maintain your calcium stores is just one of the many lies that you and your health professionals were taught to believe.*

Act 3

So can this get any worse than a loss of precious calcium? When our lifestyle choices cause our blood to become acidic, as it does when we have high levels of phosphates in it, there's a price to pay. As I mentioned earlier, acidic blood is very corrosive and corrosive blood does massive damage to the lining of your arteries, and especially to the high-flow arteries around your heart. The blood starts to wear away at the walls of the arteries.

When your brain gets the information through the nervous system that the artery walls are starting to get damaged, it doesn't just send out calcium. The brain also sends out an order to the liver to create a substance to patch the damaged areas of the arteries. That substance is called low-density lipoprotein or LDL. Then the liver sends the LDL out into the bloodstream to patch and protect the damaged areas of the arteries. If you continue to do damage, the brain is going to continue to tell the liver to produce more and more LDL independent of your diet having ANY cholesterol in it, which causes a common problem, called plaquing of your arteries.

You should note here that *high cholesterol levels are not hereditary.* They are an adaptive response by your brain to protect you from your lifestyle choices.

It might seem overwhelming to think that a choice we make, which we have been taught is good for us, is causing an adaptive response that contributes to the number one killer in the United States, heart disease. Remember what we said at the beginning; in order to expect a different result you must change your state of mind and think differently. *You are what you think.*

Now that you understand how important it is to make good choices, I am going to present what I call the four pillars of good health. These choices are the foundation of good health and well-being.

The Four Pillars of Good Health

Pillar #1: Hydration

Think of what you need to survive, really just survive. Food? Water? Air? I'm going to concentrate on water here. Water is one of the most basic things that we need to maintain our health and well-being, and it amazes me that the average American consumes less than four glasses of water per day. Water is of major importance to all living things; in some organisms, up to 90% of their body weight comes from water. Up to 60% of the human body is water, the brain is composed of 70% water, and the lungs are nearly 90% water. Lean muscle tissue contains about 75% water by weight, body fat contains 10% water, and bone has 22% water. About 83% of our blood is water, which helps digest our food, transport waste, and control body temperature. You should be drinking ½ of your body weight in ounces of water per day. For instance, if you weigh 120 pounds you should be drinking 60 ounces of water. Just making that one choice alone will help you heal, decrease pain, improve muscle function, and detoxify.

The most common question here is, what qualifies as a glass of water? You can naturally flavor your water with a 5% juice. Decaffeinated tea is also considered a glass of water, but coffee or tea with caffeine is not. Make sure that you are drinking your water at room temperature, and ideally it should be spring or filtered water.

Pillar #2: Sleep

Sleep is one of the most essential pillars of life. Your body does 80% of its healing at night. When your body needs to heal or is out of balance, your brain causes you to be tired or have a lack of energy. Seems like a simple fact, but it is estimated that 50% of Americans are sleep deprived. The average person requires eight hours of sleep per night—how much are you getting?

What few people know is that it's even more important to set your sleep periods at a consistent time. If you are able to go to bed and wake up at the same time every night, you can get away with less sleep. Equally important is the quality of those hours of sleep. If you're giving yourself plenty of time for sleep but still having trouble waking up in the morning or staying alert all day, you may not be spending enough time in the different stages of sleep— especially deep sleep and REM sleep. By understanding how the sleep cycles work and the factors that can lead to those cycles being disrupted, you'll be able to start getting both the quantity and the quality of sleep you need.

Chinese medicine identifies that your body has two energy spikes: one at noon and one at midnight. These energy spikes are when your nervous system is functioning most efficiently. You should be in your deep sleep cycle before you go into your midnight energy spike in order to get the maximum amount of healing for your body, which means you should be in bed two hours before midnight.

Two of the most common questions that I get in practice are "What position should I sleep in?" and "What kind of pillow should I use?"

"What position should I sleep in?"

To answer these questions correctly, I'll start by talking about something called surface area and pressure points. Sleep is the only time your body should be in one position for hours at a time. In order for you to be comfortable, you should choose a position which disperses your weight over the greatest amount of surface area to decrease weight on your pressure points. That position is on your back, not your side. Your side has the smallest surface area, which means more weight on pressure points. You'll toss and turn all night.

"What kind of pillow should I use?"

It is also extremely important to choose the correct pillow. A pillow should be able to keep your neck in a neutral position (in line with your body) with the support under your neck, not your head. It is very important to note that *the pillow is for your neck*. So the softer the pillow, the better it is. I recommend a 500–750 down pillow. If you are allergic to down pillows, a good alternative is a water pillow. You can control the amount of firmness by adjusting the amount of water that you put into the pillow.

Pillar #3: You Are What You Eat, The ABC's Of Nutrition

It's impossible to reach your maximum health potential unless you "eat for life." What does this mean? Eating the right things at the right times. Included in this section are nutritional guidelines for you to read and follow for life. Eating strategically will allow for maximum digestion and absorption, and will give you all of the energy you'll need throughout your day. I have put together a summary of the guidelines that I use for my patients when it comes to eating right. For more nutritional information, go to AtlantisWellness.com.

Nutritional Guidelines

Combining Foods:

Certain foods don't digest very well together. Use the following as a rule for food consumption.

Proteins require acidic gastric juices, whereas starches require alkaline (basic) ph levels. This is why starches (breads, pastas, potatoes) and proteins should be eaten at separate meals. You should decide whether your meal is a "protein" or a "starch" meal and then combine either with a vegetable.

As far as eating fruit goes, there is a rule: "Eat it alone or leave it alone."

The Morning Routine:

The following is a list of different foods that can and should be eaten for breakfast, but obviously not all at once. This is strategic nutrition at its best. It allows for maximum energy and production.

- Fresh fruit and fruit juices (always use fresh if you can)
- Fresh vegetable juices and salads
- Kashi Organic Promise cereal with (soy or rice milk)
- Grains (oatmeal is ideal)
- *No cow's milk*
- Switch to Ezekiel bread or a sprouted grain bread

The Afternoon Routine:

Maintaining high energy for the most strenuous part of the day is important. This diet allows for your body to effectively eliminate waste and toxins and give you "the steam" to make it through the rest of the day.

1. *Do not overeat!*
2. *Do not combine water or other liquids with your food—it weakens the strength of the acid in your stomach.*
3. Eat a salad for lunch whenever possible. Avoid dressings with lots of fat, chemicals, salt, or sugar. Salad is water rich and cleanses the intestines. The veggies will give you lots of energy for the rest of the day.
4. Eating fruit or fruit salad is a great lunch.
5. If not salad, wheat pasta. Use a light sauce. No butter or heavy meat sauce. Use a light marinara with little salt and sugar.
6. Try not to eat foods with a lot of chemical additives, preservatives, sugar, or MSG. These are all toxins to the body.
7. Do not eat cake, cookies, or sweets with lots of sugar after lunch.
8. Eating onions or garlic will not only make your breath stink, it will also cause you to crave large amounts of food.
9. *Do not* eat a lot of bread with lunch, and if you eat any, eat only sprouted grain bread.

10. Eat as little dairy as possible, it creates phlegm and has lots of chemicals.

11. Always wait about 25 minutes after lunch before eating a piece of fruit.

Snacking:

When snacking during the day, try to eat fruits and/or vegetables. You can also eat small amounts of dry cereal (without a lot of sugar), hard pretzels, nuts, seeds, raisins, or other "natural" desserts.

More Rules of Nutrition:

These are some rules to follow when planning a diet for you or your family. These will help you and those you care about to be healthy, energetic human beings.

1. Eat many small meals (about six) throughout the day. This will allow you to maintain a higher level of insulin, therefore burning more fat, as well as maintaining a higher, more constant level of energy.

2. Always eat slowly, and breathe while you eat. Chew your food well, and relax.

3. Only eat when you are hungry. Allow yourself to be physically full. This means that you should recognize when you're physically satisfied. Don't just eat because fifteen minutes ago you were "starving." Eat until you are full and then stop.

4. Sugar has many different names: dextrose, sucrose, fructose, corn syrup, brown sugar, or corn sweeteners. If any one of these names is one of the first four ingredients in a food, chances are it is highly processed and not worth buying.

5. Eat meat (which includes red meat, chicken, turkey, or fish) in very small quantities. Always trim the visible fat off meats before cooking.

6. Eat dairy, saturated fats, and foods high in cholesterol sparingly. Instead, eat polyunsaturated fats and fry foods as little as possible.
7. Limit the amount of canned or processed foods, as they have too many additives and preservatives.
8. Consistency of good nutrition is what will make you a toxin-free bundle of energy.
9. If the amount of fat in a particular food is more than 1/3 the total amount of calories—don't eat or buy that food.
10. Most of all, use *common sense* when "eating for life."

Pillar #4: Balance your nervous system with chiropractic

We started this chapter talking about holding yourself accountable for your lifestyle choices. Sadly, most people wait until it is too late to make the decision to get healthy. In fact, most people judge their health based on symptoms. This is how the medical and pharmaceutical professions want you to think. There is more money ($70 billion) in treating the problem than in preventing it. Unfortunately, symptoms are the last sign your body gives you to tell you that something is wrong. It's like having a bad shingle on your roof: You don't know you have a bad roof until you see the stain on your ceiling. That is why waiting for symptoms to appear is the worst way to take care of yourself and your family. Fact: A cavity usually doesn't hurt for two years. Fact: Cancer usually doesn't hurt at all, until the end. Fact: 36% of all heart attack victims have their fatal heart attack as their very first symptom.

Chiropractic care allows your body to function at its highest level, and can prevent problems from developing in the first place. Just like brushing your teeth will prevent tooth decay, maintaining a healthy, strong spine will prevent spinal decay.

Your spine is protected by 24 moveable vertebrae (which act like circuit breakers) and the spinal nerves exit between each vertebra and go out to deliver the messages sent from the brain to each muscle, gland, organ, and cell in your body. As long as there is no interference to your brain, spinal cord, and spinal nerves, your body has the ability to function at its optimum level...in other words, as close to 100% as possible. When there is interference, it causes the body to malfunction and interferes with the body's ability to adapt to the stress that you are exposing your body to due to your lifestyle.

Here's how chiropractic works:

Chiropractic is the only healing profession in the world that recognizes that your body has the ability to function at its optimum level, as long as there is no interference to the master control system (the nervous system). Makes sense, don't you think? A chiropractor's job is to locate, analyze, and remove any interference to the nervous system. These blockages or misalignments are called *vertebral subluxations*. When a spinal nerve is being choked because of a vertebral subluxation, the muscle, organ, or gland that is attached to it cannot receive all of the information that the brain is trying to send to it. A study by Dr. Seth Sharpless at the University of Colorado has shown that brain impulses can be decreased up to 60% by placing the weight of a dime on a nerve. Our bodies cannot react and function properly at 40%.

When a circuit overloads in your house and it "blows," you go down to the breaker box and check all of the circuits. You examine all of them to make sure they are in alignment, and when you come to the one that is out of alignment, you simply click the circuit and turn the power back on. The body works in the same way. A chiropractor simply checks your spine to make sure that all of the vertebrae are in perfect alignment. When a vertebra is out of alignment, a situation referred to as a subluxation, it can be adjusted by the doctor's hands so that the "power" can be turned back on to the muscle, organ, or gland that the nerve controls.

> *A body that is free of nerve interference has more power to heal, think, and metabolize. 90% of the stimulation and nutrition to the brain is generated by movement of the spine."*
>
> —*Dr. Roger Sperry,*
> *Nobel Prize winner for brain research*

Conclusion

I hope that by reading this it has stimulated you to think a little differently about maintaining your health and well-being. Health starts from within. Your health is a product of your body adapting to your lifestyle choices. To maximize your true potential, it is vital to maintain a healthy functioning nervous system and to make sure that you hold yourself accountable for your lifestyle choices. Live long and be well. Good luck!

Questions and Activities for Maintaining Your Optimal Health

Write out your top five Personal Goals and top five Health Goals.

List five action steps under each that you will have to do to achieve them.

What effects are your lifestyle habits having on your health and wellness?

Where are you getting your information about the choices that are driving your actions?

What are five decisions that you can make today that will allow you to be healthier tomorrow?

What are the first steps you can take to add more nutrients to your diet?

What is the single most defining characteristic of your health and well-being?

How many glasses of water should you drink per day? How many do you drink?

How many hours of sleep do you get per night? How many should you get?

Can milk actually cause bone loss?

About the Author

Dr. Peter Martone is the owner and director of Atlantis Chiropractic Wellness Centers, and an international speaker on Health and Wellness. For over 12 years, his mission has been to make Massachusetts the healthiest place to live on the planet by guiding people through his Interactive Healing Experience.

Dr. Martone's techniques have been featured nationally on CBS news multiple times. Dr. Martone is also co-host for a new TV show called "Body, Mind and Spirit"—dedicated to empowering people with information in order for them to make informed lifestyle change.

CHAPTER 6:

THE INS AND OUTS OF RETIREMENT LIVING AND SENIOR CARE

Erwin and Kate Allado,
SeniorCareHomes.com

Familiarizing yourself with different types of senior housing options is important when planning for your retirement. Having a better understanding of all the available options can definitely make the process much easier and less stressful. Read on to learn about the types of senior housing and care home options for seniors.

Types of Retirement Communities

Independent Living

Independent Living Communities, also referred to as Retirement Communities, are for individuals from the ages of 55 and up. This senior housing option is ideal for healthy and active seniors who want to live independently with flexibility in their day-to-day activities. Seniors who choose Independent Living typically do not need medical assistance.

Independent Living communities usually offer a wide range of personal services to seniors, such as cleaning, laundry, transportation to church and shopping, outings, group meals, fitness programs, etc.

Continuing Care Retirement Communities

Continuing Care Retirement Communities are senior care facilities that are typically referred to as CCRCs or life care retirement communities. This senior housing option is perfect for seniors who want to age in the same place. They offer flexible accommodations that are intended to meet the needs and wants of seniors. Although care needs may change over time for a resident, this type of facility avoids the worry about moving.

Continuing Care Retirement Communities offer a long-term continuing care contract, usually for a resident's lifetime. They provide appropriate levels of senior care support for independent living, assisted living, or nursing care, all in one facility. Although CCRCs can be pricey, this senior housing option is becoming one of the most popular choices today because it conveniently offers a wide range of available programs, activities, and amenities to support the healthy lifestyle of seniors.

Payment Options

The costs related to independent living are determined by the location, size, amenities, and types of services needed by the senior. The monthly rate for a one-bedroom apartment in a retirement community can be as low as $1400 per month or as high as $5500 per month (costs may also be higher in major metropolitan areas).

Typically, a retirement community charges a one-time, non-refundable community fee, also known as an admission fee. This can range anywhere from $1000 to $5000 depending on the type of contract, and it's due upon admittance.

The most popular types of payment options available for retirement communities are Pay-as-you-go and the Buy-in option.

- Pay-as-you-go is a contract that is basically a straight rental agreement. This is the most popular payment option for retirement communities, since it doesn't involve an investment or down payment. However, be careful, because monthly rents may be subject to price increases. Under this payment plan, the resident may also pay a non-refundable entrance fee.
- The Buy-in option may include entrance fees and monthly payments, depending on the terms of the contract. This type of payment option offers ownership to the residents and allows residents to purchase their own living area.

How to Find the Communities

Searching for a retirement community may take some time. The best way to begin the search will be to determine what you can realistically afford. It may be a waste of time to tour different communities that have the amenities and preferences you want if they are not within your budget.

After determining your budget, you'll have to decide on the area you want to move to. Be sure to consider the distance of the community from your doctor, relatives, and other places you need to visit. Then make a priority list of items and activities you would like to find in retirement communities that are important for your happiness and well-being.

By knowing your budget, location, and other preferences, you will be prepared and ready to search for the right retirement community. There are three ways to find a community:

1. Online: You can surf the web for online directories that provide listings of retirement communities in your area or other desired locations.

2. Referral or Placement Services: The most reliable way is to talk to your family and friends about retirement communities and ask if they have any recommendations. You may also visit senior centers to get listings of retirement communities in the area. Be sure to talk to the staff members and/or senior participants for suggestions. Don't forget to consult with local placement agencies like SeniorCareHomes.com, as they will have the details for the communities in the area of your choice.

3. Offline: You can check newspapers and magazines for listings, or you can go to a pharmacy, grocery, or local hospital to get a free copy of retirement living directories.

Downsizing & Moving Tips

Downsizing one's home can be very demanding physically, mentally, and emotionally, as it involves a lot of planning, packing, and letting go of emotional ties to the home.

The decision to downsize is not an easy one, especially with all the memories shared in the home over the years. Most would agree that packing is still the most challenging aspect when one downsizes. It will be very tough to decide on which things to bring and which things to throw away, leave, or sell. One has to accept that the new home will be smaller; therefore, it is impossible to bring all the things that have been accumulated over the years. Here are some tips to make downsizing easier and less stressful:

1. Check the Layout of the New Place: To help downsize, it will be good to find out in advance the layout for the new place so you know how much space you will have. This will help you and your loved one decide on what will fit and which items you can bring.

2. Sort Wisely: Avoid clutter by separating the things that you barely use or do not need at all.

3. One Room at a Time: When packing, start with rooms you use the least, as they will have less emotional attachments.

4. Keep a List: Downsizing can be overwhelming, as there are tons of things to do. In order to stay organized, it is important to keep a list so you don't forget anything.

5. Sort: Determine the things to keep, give to family and friends, sell/donate, or throw away.

6. Take Pictures: It's a good idea to take pictures of important items you leave behind. This might make the "letting go" process easier.

7. Where is the New Place? If you will be moving to an assisted living facility, cooking utensils and dinner plates will no longer be needed. Donating them to social services or other charitable organizations is a good option.

8. Relax: Everything is done! You can now relax with your loved one. If you are helping someone else, assure him or her that he or she made the right choice to downsize.

Moving and Settling in

Moving is one of the most stressful events for seniors, as it involves a lot of time and emotions. Staying organized is key in preventing a stressful move.

With so many things to do, it will be helpful to make a moving checklist of things to remember, like transferring your prescription(s), filing a change of address with the post office, calling your utility service companies to schedule disconnection for your old house and a connection date for your new place, etc.

Organizing and packing items room-by-room will make the packing process easier. Be sure to also label all the boxes. This way all your things won't get mixed up, thus making it easier to unpack and find things once you settle into your new place.

Making Friends and Enriching Your Stay

Having an active social life can help extend a person's life and provide numerous benefits physically, mentally, and emotionally. Socialization in retirement communities is very important, as it helps seniors stay active while also making new friends.

Studies show that people in a retirement community who stay active and social tend to remain happier and healthier compared to those who do not. Maintaining friendships with people who share the same interests promotes contentment and self-esteem, as it helps residents retain a general sense of purpose.

Usually, retirement communities provide an atmosphere that encourages residents to socialize with each other. As a new resident, it is good to participate in different activities and social gatherings in order to meet other residents that share the same interests and values. Joining different clubs and activities like scrapbooking, gardening, playing bingo, movie nights, or other social activities is a great way to make new friends.

My Loved One's Care Guide & My Future

When is it Time to Transition to Senior Housing?

Are you worried about mom or dad living alone? Don't know if assisted living is right for your aging parent? Finding a good Assisted Living Facility that matches the senior's needs can be time-consuming and very challenging.

Here are 10 signs to help you determine when to start the Senior Housing search. Familiarizing yourself with these signs will help make the planning process and the Senior Housing transition easier and less stressful for seniors and their families.

10 Signs That It's Time to Start the Senior Housing Search

1. Mobility Issues: Is your aging parent having trouble walking around the house or walking up and down the stairs, or demonstrating any signs of decreased mobility? Are you worried about falls and fractures due to normal physical changes that can limit your loved one's mobility? If your answer is yes, then it may be time to start the Senior Housing search to ensure the safety of your aging loved one.

2. Memory Problems: Do mom or dad tend to forget important events or doctor appointments, or to take medications? Do you notice any issues related to memory problems, like repeating the same questions and statements over and over, misplacing things, or leaving the stove on several times? Does your aging loved one wander away from home? If yes, you might want to start the Senior Housing search before a crisis happens.

3. Needs Help with Personal Care or Grooming: Does your aging parent go without brushing his/her hair, wear dirty clothes, have bad breath, or demonstrate other signs of neglecting personal hygiene? For seniors with medical conditions, hygienic tasks may be difficult to do. Typically, senior housing facilities provide assistance with activities of daily living, which includes bathing, toileting, dressing, and more.

4. Housekeeping Issues: Next time you visit your aging loved one, look around the house. Is the house well maintained? Are the counters and floors dirty? Are there spoiled foods in the refrigerator? Assistance with household chores is usually provided for seniors who live in senior housing facilities.

5. Driving Safety Issues: Are you worried about your aging loved one's driving abilities? Are there scratches or dents on the car or several traffic tickets? These driving safety issues may be a result of cognitive impairment and diminished motor capabilities due to aging. If you feel that your parent or aging relative can no longer drive safely, you have to find a way to get him or her to stop driving. You may want to consider moving your aging loved one to a senior housing facility, as they provide transportation services to senior residents.

6. Weight Loss: Has your mom, dad, or aging relative been losing weight? Is it a sudden weight loss? If yes, then it might be an indication that the senior is not eating. This may be due to a decrease in appetite, or loss of ability to do grocery shopping, or to prepare and cook their own food.

7. Money Management Assistance: When visiting your aging relative, do you notice tons of bills on the counter, receipts for large charitable donations, or calls or final notices from creditors? Daily money management assistance may also be offered in different senior housing facilities.

8. Issues with Medication: Proper medication is important for seniors who have medical conditions. When visiting your aging relative, do you notice any expired medicine bottles or unfilled prescriptions? If you do, this may be a sign that your aging loved one is no longer able to manage his or her own medications properly. Keep in mind that medications are essential to prevent or treat illnesses, especially for seniors.

9. Inability to Communicate: Does your aging loved one experience difficulties in communicating their feelings and emotions? If yes, then it might be a sign that your elderly loved one is starting to lose the sharpness she or he once had. Keep in mind that communication is very important, especially for seniors. When seniors are not able to clearly express themselves, they tend to be frustrated.

10. Depression: Decreased interest in activities your aging loved one once enjoyed, moodiness, lack of appetite, fatigue, and other behavioral changes are some signs of depression. Early detection is key in order to keep your aging loved ones safe. If you are not able to monitor your aging relative, then assisted living is a good option to ensure senior safety.

Start the Senior Housing Conversation Early

Don't wait for a crisis to happen or to see your aging parents start to decline before talking about senior housing. Express your concerns about their safety, health, and being alone. It is also important that you ask them open-ended questions, get their ideas, and understand their worries.

It is common to feel uncomfortable at first when talking to your parents about senior housing, but remember it's better to let them know their senior care options so they can be involved in the decision-making process. This will allow you to get feedback about what your parents think when the time comes. This will give you peace of mind, as you will already know what your parents want for their future.

Preparing Aging Parents for Senior Housing

Talking about senior housing with your parents is probably one of the most difficult conversations you will ever have. Some seniors may not like to entertain the fact that someday assisted living care or other types of senior care options will be needed. They obviously don't want to lose their independence. But remember that their safety and needs are the number one priority. How can you start the conversation with your parents about senior housing? What are the things that you should consider when talking about senior housing? Here are a few tips to keep in mind.

Discussing Senior Housing with Aging Loved Ones

Aging is inevitable. At some point in our lives, each one of us will need help with Activities of Daily Living due to aging or a medical condition. It is very important to start the conversation with your aging parent about senior housing sooner rather than later. It may be difficult to talk about the possibility of a senior housing option, but it's best to talk to your aging parents while they are still in good health.

Family Decision

Holidays or family parties are an ideal time to discuss with the family what's best for Mom and Dad, since everyone is together. It is ideal to get siblings and immediate family members involved, as taking care of the elderly loved one is a family decision and responsibility.

If you have siblings, be sure to talk to them first and brainstorm with them about the senior housing option before talking to your aging parents about it. If you all come to agreement that senior housing is the best care option for your mom or dad, you can start talking about the game plan. Decide on the time, date, place, and who will initiate the assisted living talk with your parents.

Keep the Assisted Living Conversation Private

Plan on talking to your parents about senior housing during a private moment in a comfortable setting. Try to keep it to a select few. You do not want your aging parents to feel threatened or embarrassed in front of everyone. Keeping it intimate and more personal during a private time will allow your parents to be more open about discussing the possibility of senior housing.

Be Positive. Focus on the Senior Housing Benefits.

For some, Assisted Living or other types of senior housing facilities may have a negative connotation. Be sure to emphasize the positive aspects, focusing on how a senior housing facility can help keep your aging parent safe and secure. Talk to them about the different social and recreational activities, food, and friends they'll meet, as well as the other services that they'll enjoy.

You might also want to take them to a nearby facility that offers lunch, so they can put aside any misconceptions. Assure them that you will find the right senior housing facility that will suit their lifestyle when the time comes.

Research About Assisted Living

Once you decide to talk to your aging parents about senior housing, be sure to come prepared. It's important to do your research to familiarize yourself with the pros and cons of senior housing facilities.

As previously mentioned, remember to start the senior housing conversation early and don't hold off. Too often families wait until the last minute, which makes the entire process rushed and stressful. Under time pressure, you're forced to make rash decisions, thus not being able to thoroughly weigh all of your options. Just like raising children, there is no "perfect way" or one-way approach. However, if you prepare for it and give yourself enough time, finding the right senior housing will be a lot easier for everyone involved.

How to Find Care

Choosing the right senior housing for your aging loved one is a big decision and one that can be very stressful. Narrowing down your choices by care needs, budget, and location will help make the search for senior housing much easier.

Consider different sources when searching for possible senior housing facilities. Friends and families who can give recommendations may be the most reliable source. You can also surf the web to find online directories for senior housing facilities in your area, which may be the easiest and most convenient way of finding possible senior care facilities. Using online sites like SeniorCareHomes. com gives you access to local senior housing listings that can be sorted by type, location, services, and price.

Checking local and regional newspapers, especially the Sunday edition, will also be helpful.

Moving to a senior care facility is a big change for both you and your aging loved one, and having support during this difficult transition will be helpful. By seeking the guidance of a social worker or a local senior care placement agency, you will make it much easier to plan for the move.

Factors That Determine Senior Housing Fees

Keep in mind that prices of each senior care facility may vary depending on the specifications you are looking for. You will have to decide on the following:

1. Level of care: The higher the level of care needed, the more costly it will be.

2. Type of facility: This depends on the type of senior care facility needed (i.e. assisted living, nursing home, residential care home, etc.). Typically, nursing homes are more expensive because of the residents' medical needs.

3. Location: The senior housing cost will also depend on the location you prefer. Usually facilities in major metropolitan areas tend to be more expensive.

4. Amenities: Some senior care facilities offer recreational/social activities and some do not. Additional services like laundry, banking, transportation services, etc. may be available for an added fee.

5. Additional Services: When additional help with eating, bathing, toileting, grooming, dressing, and other personal and medical services are needed on a daily basis.

Types of Care

Finding the right senior housing option, whether an assisted living facility, a nursing home, or another type senior care facility, can be overwhelming at first. However, having a better understanding of all the available senior housing options in your area will make it easier and less stressful.

Assisted Living

Other common terms: Residential Care for the Elderly (RCFE)

Assisted Living Facilities are suited for seniors who want to live independently but need help with day-to-day activities. Seniors who select this senior housing option do not require 24-hour supervision, since they do not have any serious medical conditions.

Assisted Living Facilities typically offer meal service, housekeeping, social activities for seniors, medication assistance, transportation for medical appointments, and other pleasure trips for seniors. Additional services like laundry, assistance with eating, bathing, toileting, grooming, dressing and other personal care may also be available in an Assisted Living Facility.

In general, Assisted Living Facilities are not required to have nurses and/or doctors 24 hours a day, seven days a week, although they usually have medical staff on site or on call to help seniors with their daily needs.

> **Payment Source:** *Mostly private pay, long-term care insurance, some may accept Medicaid or other government-sponsored programs.*
> **Price Range:** *$1800 to $5000 per month*

Nursing Homes or Skilled Nursing Facilities

Commonly referred to as SNFs, which is short for Skilled Nursing Facilities.

Nursing Homes or Skilled Nursing Facilities provide round-the-clock nursing care for seniors with serious medical conditions.

Nursing Homes offer services from a registered nurse, licensed vocational nurse, and/or certified nursing aide 24 hours a day, seven days a week. The majority of nursing homes offer short-term and long-term care depending on the degree of care the senior residents need.

> **Payment Source:** *Private pay, long-term care insurance, Medicaid, Medicare or other government-sponsored programs.*
> **Price Range:** *$3800 to $8500 per month*

Alzheimer's Care

Other common terms: Assisted Living, Residential Care for the Elderly (RCFE)

Alzheimer's Care Facilities are also known as memory care facilities or dementia facilities. These types of senior care facilities specialize in the treatment and care of people with Alzheimer's and dementia.

The setting in Alzheimer's Care Facilities is similar to Assisted Living communities. Alzheimer's Care Facilities also provide personal services like help with eating, bathing, toileting, grooming, dressing, etc. Social activities and memory-specific programs are tailored to provide senior residents with as much mental and memory stimulation as possible.

Alzheimer's Care Facilities have 24-hour support, a higher level of security to protect wanderers, and structured programs to meet the needs of people with dementia.

> **Payment Source:** *Private pay, long-term care insurance,*

some may accept Medicaid or other government-sponsored programs.
Price Range: *$3000 to $8000 per month*

Board and Care

Other common terms: Residential Care Home (6-Bed Care Home)

Board and Care Facilities are commonly referred to as residential care facilities or convalescent homes. This senior care housing option for the elderly provides 24-hour non-medical assistance with day-to-day activities such as eating, toileting, bathing, grooming, walking, and laundry. Nursing services and additional services may also be available.

Typically, this kind of senior housing option offers a home-like setting and provides private or shared rooms, private or shared bathrooms, meal service, and an open-door policy for the senior residents' friends and family.

Payment Source: *Private pay, long-term care insurance, some may accept Medicaid or other government-sponsored programs.*
Price Range: *$1800 to $3500 per month*

In-Home Care

Other common terms: Home Care, Domiciliary care.

The term In-Home Care is used to describe a non-medical service provided in the comfort of one's own home. Some of the services available for In-Home Care include:

- Activities of Daily Living—eating, bathing, toileting, dressing, and other personal care services
- Homemaking—cleaning, laundry, cooking
- Companionship
- Transportation for shopping, banking, etc.

Industry research and studies indicate that the costs related to In-Home Care can be more expensive compared to moving an elderly person to an Assisted Living or Nursing Home. This of course depends on the senior's health condition, daily needs, and whether medical services are required. However, it is advisable to compare care options and prices for senior housing in your area so you can make the best decision for you or your aging loved one.

> *Payment Source: Private pay, long-term care insurance, Medicare, Medicaid, or other government-sponsored programs.*
>
> *Price Range: Typically home care providers or caregivers are paid on an hourly basis.*

Payment Options

Senior housing costs can vary quite a bit depending on your preferences, like the type of care, additional senior services needed, and the location you desire.

In order to plan accordingly, it is very important to know your available financing options so you can prepare for the cost of senior care. To help you understand the different financing options available for you and your family, please refer to the Care-giving Payment Options chart on the following pages.

Figure 5:
Care-Giving Payment Options
source: medicare.gov

Financing Options	Only Available for Long-Term Care	Remaining Funds Available to Heirs	Rate of Asset Growth	Eligibility Needed	Risk of Insufficient Funds	Cost
Family Support and Care-giving	No	No	None	No	Moderate: Family members may be unable / unwilling to provide care	You pay for services that family members are unable to provide
Personal Savings	No	Yes	Variable	No	High: Long-Term Care costs can exceed your personal savings	You are responsible for creating private savings
Long-Term Care Insurance	Yes	No	Fixed	Yes	Moderate to Low: Long-Term Care costs could exceed original amount	Monthly premiums for the life of the policy
Limited Long-Term Care Insurance	Yes	No	Fixed	Yes	Moderate to Low: Long-Term Care costs could exceed original coverage amount	Large one-time or short-term monthly premium
Life Settlement	Yes	No	Fixed	Yes	Moderate to Low: Amount received from benefit may not pay all long-term care costs	None
Accelerated Death Benefit	Yes	No	Fixed	Yes	Moderate to Low: Amount received from benefit may not pay all long-term care costs	None
Viatical Settlement	Yes	No	Fixed	Yes	Moderate to Low: Amount received from benefit may not pay all long-term care costs	None

Financing Options	Only Available for Long-Term Care	Remaining Funds Available to Heirs	Rate of Asset Growth	Eligibility Needed	Risk of Insufficient Funds	Cost
Reverse Mortgage	No	Yes	Variable	Yes	Moderate: Amount received from benefit may not pay all long-term care costs. Home maintenance costs still exist	Processing and origination fees to establish mortgage
Continuing Care Retirement Community	Yes	Yes	Variable	Yes	Low: Additional care provided as needed in CCRC assisted living or nursing facility	High purchase price and fixed monthly payment required of CCRC property
Veterans Benefits	No	No	None	Yes	Moderate to High: Amount received from benefit may not pay all long-term care costs	None
Medicare	No	No	None	Yes	Moderate to High: Amount received from Medicare may not pay all long-term care costs	Co-payments and deductibles
Medicaid	No	No	None	Yes	High: Amount received from Medicaid may not pay all long-term care costs. Recovery of Medicaid may be made against estate	You pay for services not covered by Medicaid
PACE	Yes	No	None	Yes	Moderate to High: Amount received from benefit may not pay all long-term care costs	You pay for services not covered by PACE

Weighing Options/Evaluating Housing Needs

Selecting the right senior housing facility is important in order to avoid moving your aging loved one from one senior care facility to another. The initial move to a senior care home or community will be a big adjustment, so make sure you carefully choose the best senior housing facility for your loved one. Stick to these seven tips to help increase your chances of success.

Seven Tips When Selecting a Senior Housing Facility or Community

1. Time is Your Friend: The more time you have to research available senior housing facilities in your area, the better. Also, note that senior housing vacancies can change at a moment's notice. When you are ready to move your loved one, give the senior care facility two to three weeks' advance notice.

2. Know Your Options: Get at least two or three senior housing options to compare and consider what you like the most and like the least. Are they a match for your 1) location, 2) budget, and 3) care needs? Contact a Senior Care Advisor/Expert at an Assisted Living Placement Agency like SeniorCareHomes.com. They provide free senior care options to the community based on those three factors mentioned above.

3. Talk to the Residents: Are they sociable? Are their alert levels similar to that of your loved one? Would your loved one interact well with the current senior housing residents?

4. Talk to the Owner and the Staff: Do they seem like they care? Do they take time with you or rush you off? How do they interact with the residents and residents' family members?

5. References: Get opinions from the residents' family members.

6. Just the Facts: How long ago did they open their first senior housing facility, and how long have they been in the senior care industry? Do they have any major state licensing citations?

7. Observe: How clean is the facility? Does it smell good or bad? Do they display pictures of events or celebrations of the residents and their families in the senior housing facility (or have an album)? Do they post their food menu or schedule of activities? Are the residents left alone in their room to do nothing?

Government Agencies and Other Resources

VA Aid and Attendance for Assisted Living

The Veterans Administration offers a special pension called Aid and Attendance that helps pay for care in an assisted living or nursing home facility. This VA benefit is largely unknown and often overlooked by families of veterans or surviving spouses of veterans who need financial assistance.

The Veterans Administration Aid and Attendance Program for Senior Housing

One of the limitations of Medicare and Medicaid is that while they provide assistance for nursing home costs, they do not provide coverage for most assisted living expenses. The cost of an assisted living facility can be very expensive, which makes it unaffordable for many seniors.

For veterans and their spouses who are entering their later years and would like to explore assisted living options, the Veterans Administration may be able to provide assistance through the VA Aid and Attendance Program. The VA Aid and Attendance benefit is available to qualifying veterans or surviving spouses of veterans, and helps pay for long-term health care expenses.

Qualifying for VA Aid

To qualify for the VA Aid and Attendance Special Pension for Assisted Living program, a veteran must:

- Have served in the Armed Forces on active duty for at least 90 days
- Have served at least one day of active duty during time of war
- Have received an honorable discharge
- Require assistance with activities of daily living such as bathing, eating, dressing, and walking (or the qualifying veteran's spouse must require such assistance)

Application Process for VA Aid and Attendance Benefit

Those who want to apply for this program must file a Veteran's Application for Pension or Compensation, which is available online or at any local VA office. Applicants will be asked to provide the following information or documents to the VA:

- A medical evaluation from a physician testifying to their (or their spouse's) need for special assistance
- A description of current medical conditions
- Net income
- Records establishing the veteran's net worth
- Information about recent out-of-pocket medical expenses
- A copy of the veteran's discharge papers

Each year, Congress sets an annual pension limit. The amount of pension that veterans are eligible for is determined by subtracting their current income minus any deductions (for example, recent un-reimbursed medical expenses) from that pension limit. The resulting number is then divided by 12 to determine the monthly amount of VA aid that the applicant will receive. Needless to say, if the applicant has more income than the pension limit set by Congress, he or she will not be awarded any pension payment at all.

Generally speaking, any veteran or surviving spouse of a veteran applying for the VA Aid and Attendance program can expect to receive an answer in about five months. However, if the pension is granted, a retroactive lump sum will be awarded beginning when the Application for Pension or Compensation was received by the VA.

The maximum amount of pension money that can be awarded per month is:

- $1,644 to a veteran
- $1,056 to a surviving spouse
- $1,949 to a couple

While this will not likely cover monthly room and board costs in an assisted living facility, it can cover a good portion of assisted living expenses. In addition, this VA aid program does not affect Medicaid eligibility, and even though Medicaid does not cover everything, it can be used to pay for some medical and personal care costs accrued by those in assisted living situations.

Another benefit of the Aid and Attendance Program is that veterans and their spouses (if qualified) will be able to receive completely free medical care plus coverage for prescription drugs.

VA Aid and Attendance Empowering Veterans

Given the choice, most seniors prefer to move to an assisted living facility rather than move to a nursing home. Assisted living allows seniors to maintain a greater degree of independence, while receiving assistance with daily living activities and some medical assistance.

Unfortunately, it has been very difficult for most seniors to find the financial assistance necessary to make this kind of housing a viable option. However, thanks to the VA Aid and Attendance pension program, assisted living is now a realistic possibility for the brave men and women who have served our country.

Questions for Planning Your Retirement Living

What are the steps I should take when looking for retirement living?

What types of retirement living options are out there?

What do I need to know when I downsize my home and move into retirement living?

How much do I need to save for when I eventually need retirement and/or assisted living?

What are the financing options available for senior housing?

When is it time to transition my parents into senior housing?

What is the most appropriate type of care for my loved one?

What should I look out for when touring a potential care home or community for my loved one?

How do I convince my parents they need to move out of their home into assisted living?

What tools are available to help my family find the best assisted living for my parents?

Resources

Website:
www.seniorcarehomes.com

Videos (YouTube Channel):
www.youtube.com/user/SeniorCareHomesCom

Radio & Media:
www.seniorcarehomes.com/about-ldl/press-and-media.html

About the Author

Being a son of a doctor and growing up in the healthcare industry since his early teens, Erwin Allado has always had a passion for helping the elderly. It all began in college when Erwin was Founding Father and first president of a community service-based fraternity.

After college, Erwin joined PeopleSupport, a global leader of online customer care solutions. He was promoted to Operations Supervisor after three weeks on the job, and was then sent overseas to build-out PeopleSupport's primary call center operation.

At the age of 21, Erwin was the Department Head of Operations and played an important role in growing the center from approximately 20 to 400 employees. One of his primary responsibilities included transitioning over 20 U.S. accounts (leading Fortune 500 companies such as GE Capital, Expedia, Toyota) to the Asia center and helping it become profitable in the first year of its operation. Now the company is in 38 global locations with 38,000 employees.

After his tenure at PeopleSupport, Erwin consulted directly for the CEO of Linksys (NASDAQ: CSCO) and was key in the build-out of their customer care center in Asia. Erwin then returned to California, where he switched careers to a completely different industry. Erwin joined Beverly Hills Financial Group, a premier brokerage firm providing high-end financing for major entertainment and sports celebrities. As Vice President, Erwin built his business from the ground up and achieved numerous accolades such as "Highest Gross Sales Revenue since 2000," "Top Sales Producer," and "Hardest Worker" awards, all in the same year.

Born in Southern California, Erwin holds a bachelor of business administration degree in management information systems (MIS) from Loyola Marymount University. Erwin is married and is the proud father of two wonderful children. He volunteers his spare time to the Alzheimer's Association, Knights of Columbus, and the committees for UCI MIND, Holy Trinity Church, and Serra Catholic's Miracle Blossoms.

Erwin has been a corporate executive and entrepreneur with a proven track record building start-up companies. He uses his healthcare and internet technology talents and experience to really make a difference in the community. His mission is to help seniors and families find the best senior care and senior housing information. This is how SeniorCareHomes.com was born.

9558145R00090

Made in the USA
San Bernardino, CA
19 March 2014